WE BELIEVE
IN THE HOLY SPIRIT

A Report by
The Doctrine Commission
of the General Synod
of the Church of England

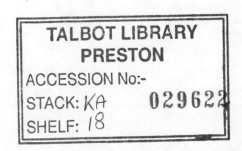

CHURCH HOUSE PUBLISHING
Church House, Great Smith Street, London SW1P 3NZ

ISBN 0 7151 3732 8

Published 1991 for the General Synod of the Church of England by Church House Publishing

Printed in England by Orphans Press Ltd., Hereford Road, Leominster, Herefordshire

Contents

Contents

Chapter 1 Introduction 1
Chapter 2 Charismatic Experience: Praying 'In the Spirit' 17
Chapter 3 Is This that? 37
Chapter 4 The Spirit of Jesus 56
Chapter 5 Spirit, Sacraments and Structures 73
Chapter 6 The Spirit and Power 92
Chapter 7 The Spirit of Truth 112
Chapter 8 The Spirit and Creation 134
Chapter 9 The Spirit and Creativity 149
Chapter 10 The Holy Spirit and the Future 170
Illustrations .... between pages 92 and 93

The Doctrine Commission
1986 – 1989

CHAIRMAN

The Right Revd John A. Baker (until 1987)
Bishop of Salisbury

The Right Revd Alec Graham (from 1987)
Bishop of Newcastle

MEMBERS

The Revd Derek Allen (until 1988)
Vicar of St Saviour and St Peter, Eastbourne; Canon and Prebendary of Chichester

The Revd Dr Paul Avis (from 1989)
Vicar of Stoke Canon, Poltimore with Huxham, and Rewe with Netherexe, Devon

The Revd Dr David Brown
Van Mildert Professor of Divinity in the University of Durham, and Canon of Durham; previously Fellow, Chaplain and Tutor of Oriel College, Oxford, and Lecturer in Theology, University of Oxford

The Right Revd Colin Buchanan
Honorary Assistant Bishop in the Diocese of Rochester; previously Bishop Suffragan of Aston

Dr Sarah Coakley
Lecturer in Religious Studies, Lancaster University

Miss Ruth Etchells
formerly Principal of St John's College, with Cranmer Hall, Durham, and Senior Lecturer in the University of Durham

The Revd Dr John Polkinghorne FRS (from 1989)
President of Queens' College, Cambridge; previously Dean of Trinity Hall, Cambridge

The Revd Dr Derek Stanesby
Canon of Windsor

The Revd Dr Anthony Thiselton
Principal of St John's College, with Cranmer Hall, Durham; previously Principal of St John's College, Nottingham, and Special Lecturer in the University of Nottingham

The Revd Dr Rowan Williams
Lady Margaret Professor of Divinity in the University of Oxford, and Canon of Christ Church

The Revd Dr Thomas Wright (from 1989)
Fellow, Chaplain and Tutor of Worcester College, Oxford, and Lecturer in Theology, University of Oxford

CONSULTANTS

The Revd Dr John Polkinghorne FRS (1988-89)
then Dean of Trinity Hall, Cambridge

The Revd Dr John Rodwell (from 1988)
Research Fellow in Biological Sciences, Lancaster University

SECRETARIES

The Revd John Meacham (until 1989)
formerly Chaplain and Research Assistant to the Bishop of Salisbury

The Revd Dr John Clark (from 1989)
Vicar of Longframlington, Northumberland

Chairman's Preface

On behalf of the Commission I wish to place on record our gratitude to several people who have given us invaluable help in the preparation of this report:

to the Bishop of Salisbury, formerly Chairman of the Commission whose creative and generous mind we have greatly missed;

to two members of the last Doctrine Commission, the Revd Dr John Barton and the Revd Dr Anthony Harvey, who have both produced preparatory papers on which we have drawn;

to the Revd Canon Michael Green and the Revd Tom Smail, who have both written notes for us in which they have drawn on their close knowledge of the charismatic movement;

to our two consultants, both of whom attended some of our meetings: the Revd Dr John Polkinghorne FRS, who, during our work on this report, became a member of the Commission; and the Revd Dr John Rodwell, to whom we are particularly indebted for much intellectual stimulus;

to our ever-loyal and efficient secretary, the Revd John Meacham, who has contributed in countless ways to the work of the Commission, who has prepared the indices to this report and whose ill-health has so greatly saddened us;

to the Revd Dr John Clark, who took over the duties of secretary in the final stages of the preparation of this report;

and to those who have given us secretarial support at our meetings, notably Miss Keri Lewis, Mrs Pauline Druiff and Mrs Doris Kay of the General Synod Office.

We Believe in the Holy Spirit

This report, like the last, *We Believe in God,* comes with the approval and agreement of the entire Commission. Each chapter was drafted by one person, who in some cases drew on material supplied by others; each chapter once drafted was considered, revised and refined by the entire Commission, a process which in the case of some chapters was repeated several times; final editorial touches were made by the Chairman. Left to ourselves, some of us might well have preferred to express certain matters rather differently, but all our members have endorsed the entire report. Also, like the last, this report is published under the authority of the House of Bishops and is commended by the House to the Church for study. It is humbly offered to the Church at large in the hope that it will enable many interested readers to believe in the Holy Spirit with deeper understanding.

ALEC NEWCASTLE

1

Introduction

The Holy Spirit may without exaggeration be called the heart-beat of the Christian, the life-blood of the Christian Church. In the second half of this century the words 'We believe in the Holy Spirit, the Lord, the giver of life' have acquired greater depth and meaning for Christian people in every tradition. The Holy Spirit has recovered a prominent place in Christian testimony and experience, in hymns and in prayers. In this study of this topical subject we seek to explore the meaning of these words from the Nicene Creed.

For the title of our work, however, we have drawn on the simpler, terser words of the Apostles' Creed, just as in 1987 the Doctrine Commission drew on the opening words of the Apostles' Creed for the title for its report, *We Believe in God*. Like its predecessor this report concentrates on the content of belief rather than on the nature of believing. It is offered to the Church to provide guidance in understanding the doctrine of the Holy Spirit and to stimulate thought, study and discussion. The authors of both reports have encountered the same difficulty: both reports are about God. God as Trinity we believe to be both hidden and revealed, mysterious and yet somehow manifested within the created order. The former report suggested ways in which the trinitarian nature of God may be understood and experienced, particularly in prayer and worship; some of these suggestions are developed in this report. With regard to belief in the triune God and particularly in the Holy Spirit there is in the scriptures and in the Church's tradition an astonishing variety and profusion of hint and assertion, of metaphor and image. These various claims and insights resist any attempt to fit them into a fully

1

coherent pattern. We have not attempted to make a comprehensive survey of such a vast and untidy subject; rather, we have tried to draw on some of the principal strands to be found concerning the Holy Spirit in the scriptures and in the Christian tradition, and to develop them in such a way as to illuminate their relationship both to one another and to certain current questions and concerns. In our work we have often been reminded that the task of theology extends beyond the handling of scripture and tradition, and that it relates to wider areas of human understanding, particularly to the natural order and to the ordering of society.

Some of these problems are not new. When Paul, for instance, came to Ephesus he found there some disciples, who told him, 'We have never even heard that there is a Holy Spirit' (Acts 19.2). Since then all instructed Christian believers and certainly all theological thinkers have heard that there is a Holy Spirit, but many Christian people have not paid much attention to the Spirit in their thinking and praying. Whitsun (or Pentecost) as a festival does not attract many more worshippers than does an ordinary Sunday, and throughout the Christian centuries theologians in general, at least in the west, have devoted surprisingly little attention to the Holy Spirit. Indeed those who have treated the Holy Spirit and the work of the Spirit have tended to discuss the influence of the Spirit in the Churches, the sacraments and the Christian life rather than to engage with the primary biblical material.

The narrative of Paul's visit to Ephesus goes on to recount how he baptized the disciples, to whom we have referred, in the name of the Lord Jesus 'and when Paul had laid his hands upon them, the Holy Spirit came on them; and they spoke with tongues and prophesied' (Acts 19.6). In every century since there have been those who, in the power of the Spirit, have prophesied and spoken in tongues, and some who have claimed that these manifestations are necessary consequences and signs of the Spirit's presence and activity. Thus against a background of relative neglect of the Holy Spirit in western Christian thinking and devotion there have been vigorous and

2

dramatic movements, from the Montanist movement of the second and third centuries to revivalist movements of the present day, which have claimed to be the sole authentic expression of the Spirit's work. Moreover, in our own day charismatic movements have deeply affected many congregations, individual worshippers, and also to some extent the entire flavour of our Church's life. These developments have been treated descriptively in two recent reports: *The Charismatic Movement in the Church of England* (1981) and *The Good Wine: Spiritual Renewal in the Church of England* by Josephine Bax (1986). Our report *We Believe in the Holy Spirit* seeks to set these particular expressions of the Spirit's work within the wider setting of the Church's life and to relate the emphases prominent in the thinking and practice of the charismatic movement to other emphases in the biblical revelation and Christian tradition.

Equally, we hope that our report will help many worshippers to appreciate and appropriate more of the riches of Christian thought and experience with regard to the Holy Spirit. Most believers have some sort of mental image of the Father and the Son, but the Spirit seems to be all the more intangible and presents greater difficulties to the imagination. Also, the self-effacing character of the Holy Spirit presents us with a particular problem, for we are told that the Holy Spirit bears witness to Christ (John 15.26). Our hope is that we enable 'ordinary churchpeople' who may or may not be caught up in the charismatic movement to think more clearly and express themselves more articulately about the very life of God in which through the Spirit they and we already share; in this connection the activity and experience of praying form a sensitive area to which we give particular attention.

It is, however, not only the ordinary, non-professional, theologically lay Christian who experiences difficulties in thinking about the Holy Spirit. These difficulties, and others too, are faced by the professional theologian. Within the last twenty years some influential figures in English theology, faced with the problem of thinking about God and with traditional trinitarian language, have reached conclusions which in effect dismantle the Trinity: language about the Holy Spirit is regarded as metaphor for divine action in the world or just as a way of referring to God, more particularly to God in relation to the world. By contrast, in common with the universal Church we maintain the appropriateness of, indeed the necessity for, traditional trinitarian belief in the Holy Spirit as a distinct mode of being or Person within the Trinity: here again it is the prayer of Jesus in Gethsemane and of Christian people through the Spirit, which is for us the area which contains the most promising and compelling insights. In the last resort 'no one comprehends the thoughts of God except the Spirit of God' (1 Cor. 2.11), but Paul is quite clear that his readers in, for instance, Galatia (Gal. 3.2) and Corinth (1 Cor. 2.12) have received the Spirit, and it is our conviction that to his language about our participation in the Spirit (2 Cor. 13.14) justice can best be done by belief in the Spirit as a distinct 'hypostasis' or Person integral to the very being of the godhead. This is discussed more fully elsewhere in this study, particularly at the end of the next chapter.

The full personhood of the Spirit within the Trinity is but one of several questions with which we are faced in thinking about the Holy Spirit. The Commission also considered the move made by some modern theologians with feminist sympathies to see the Holy Spirit as a 'feminine' principle in the Trinity. The idea has some interesting, if sporadic, support in the tradition, especially in the early Syriac patristic material, where the word for 'Spirit' is itself feminine in gender; there has also been the occasional startling, and quite spontaneous, iconographical representation of the spirit as a female figure (see Plate 2). It was generally agreed by the Commission, however, that the *compensatory* projection of one 'female' figure into the Godhead, especially where this carried uncritical assumptions about the appropriate characteristics of 'femininity' (such as being soothing, mothering, constantly available at home, or mediating between the more prominent 'male' persons of the Trinity) was indicative more of traditional assumptions about power relations between the sexes than of a positive way forward in trinitarian theology. In other words, the far-reaching consequences of feminist challenges to traditional Christian theism could not adequately be met by changing the gender associations of one Person of the Trinity.[1]

Another source of difficulty consists in the common associations of the term 'spirit'. For some the word 'spirit' evokes ideas of ghosts or of beings which are said to communicate with us from beyond the grave through mediums or various forms of physical manifestation; in this sense spirit or spirits are irreducibly material. For others the word 'spirit' is linked with certain inward features of human beings, particularly with conscience, creativity, aesthetic experience and religious awareness. In other contexts the word connotes that which binds people together in a common enterprise, in a group or movement, with a shared vision and values. With regard to the dead the word 'spirit' is often used to describe their influence which is perceptible long after their life, as one might say that the spirit of Napoleon is still felt in France to-day. Christian discourse about the Holy Spirit is different from any of these common meanings and uses of the word 'spirit'. We are dealing not with the material manifestations, nor with the purely subjective, nor with an influence which comes from Jesus and is perceptible centuries after his death, nor in some vague way with the divine, nor with something which characterizes and distinguishes humanity from the rest of the created order, nor with anything which science would classify as matter or energy.

When we turn to our Bible we find in both the Old and the New Testament a wide range of meaning for the words translated 'spirit'. So far as the Old Testament is concerned, it is arguable that the use of the word 'spirit' with reference to

---

[1]The paper by Sarah Coakley originally presented to the Commission on this theme is now published in ed. M. Furlong, *Mirror to the Church,* pp. 124-35.

God is borrowed from its use with reference to human beings, who are all animated by breath. If this is the case, 'spirit' is first applied to people and is then applied by extension to God, who has a divine, a holy spirit, not the feeble kind of spirit which we have and which deserts us at death. Spirit is breathed by God into human beings for their very life, for the empowering of individuals with respect to particular tasks, and for the activity of prophecy. Once, however, the term spirit has been applied to God, then spirit becomes that which God essentially is; those beings are most truly spiritual whose nature and existence are most completely like God, and determined by God's creative and saving power. We need also to mention that the religion of Israel needed to do justice to a faith in God who was believed to be both infinite, eternal, unapproachable, and also active here and now in human affairs, indeed in the hearts and minds of human beings. From the time of the exile onwards and especially in some of the latest parts of the Old Testament we find that terms such as the Spirit of God, like the Wisdom or Word or Law of God, are used with reference to the work of God in creating the universe and to the presence of God in sustaining it. We note that this terminology about the divine activity in creating and sustaining the universe is generally claimed by the New Testament writers for Christ, rather than for the Spirit. That is a major shift of emphasis between the two testaments, and it is this shift which in part explains why (as we have seen) some Christian thinkers find no need to treat the Holy Spirit as a distinct Person.

When we turn to the New Testament we discern both continuity and discontinuity with the Old. The New Testament writers develop many of the ideas and images used in the Old Testament. However, as we have seen, they do not hesitate in one major respect to use the language of the Old Testament in a quite different sense, a sense derived from their conviction about the centrality of Jesus Christ in God's providential design for the universe and more particularly about the centrality of the redemption wrought by him.

Within the New Testament itself there is both unity and diversity in the material concerning the Holy Spirit. We draw particular attention to two important features where there is unanimity among the New Testament authors who treat them. First, according to all four gospels the Spirit was closely associated with the baptism of Jesus, descending upon him then. The Spirit thus was understood to have in some sense inspired and empowered Jesus in his public ministry of preaching and teaching and in his performance of mighty works. His ministry reached its climax and fulfilment in his passion and crucifixion. Our understanding of the work of the Spirit is thus shaped and moulded by the course of Jesus' life and, more particularly, by his death. Further, the Spirit is believed to be powerfully at work in connection with Jesus' resurrection from the dead (Rom.1.4). Christian faith is properly Christocentric and is centred on the events of Good Friday and of Easter. This framework of reference governs our understanding of the work of the Spirit whom we believe to be the Spirit of God and of Christ. Further, we note, what may be one of the few references to the Holy Spirit in the Epistle to the Hebrews bears upon the sacrificial obedience of Christ, 'who through the eternal Spirit offered himself without blemish to God' (Heb. 9.14). In our view it is particularly significant that, in Gethsemane on the night of his betrayal to death, Jesus prayed, 'Abba, Father' (Mark 14.36), and that the only other occasion on which we find this expression in the New Testament are two passages in Paul's epistles (Rom. 8.15; Gal. 4.6) both of which deal with the work of the Spirit; in the chapters which follow, particularly in 'The Spirit of Jesus', we shall return to these passages which we consider to be of crucial importance. They establish the Christological and Christocentric viewpoint which for us is one of the principal bases for understanding the Holy Spirit. The Christological or Christocentric reference also controls the discussions in the chapter entitled, 'The Spirit and Power', in which we try to evaluate within a Christological perspective the claims to the exercise of power sometimes made by those who have become vividly aware of the Spirit's powerful operation for good in their own lives and ministries.

The second respect in which we find a common mind, or the reflection of a common pattern, among the New Testament writers lies in the conviction that the Holy Spirit is shed or spread abroad as a consequence of the death and resurrection of Christ; that it is within the life and fellowship of the Christian Church that the Spirit is, as a consequence, powerfully at work; and that the Church is the particular sphere of the Spirit's operation. This conviction was expressed most provocatively in the fourth gospel; 'as yet the Spirit had not been given, because Jesus was not yet glorified' (John 7. 39). His glorification was his being lifted up on the cross and to heaven; John 19. 30,34 may convey to us the conviction that at the moment of Jesus' death his Spirit was conveyed to his disciples; John 20.22 certainly conveys the conviction that, after Jesus had ascended to the Father, he breathed the Holy Spirit upon the disciples and that within their fellowship the Spirit is powerfully at work in the ways about which we read in the farewell discourses. From the Lukan writings a similar pattern emerges; after the death and resurrection of Jesus, the Spirit, who had been active in Jesus' ministry, was given to the founder members of the young Church on the day of Pentecost, and within the Christian Church the Spirit is at work. Indeed the work of the Spirit in the young Church, as it is presented in the Acts of the Apostles, provides striking parallels with the work of Jesus, as described in Luke's gospel; thus the conviction is conveyed that the Spirit which once rested upon Jesus is now to be found within the Christian Church. Paul, too, while he has scarcely anything to say about the ministry of Jesus, is quite clear that 'God has sent the Spirit of his Son into our hearts' (Gal. 4.6), and that this Spirit is to be found in Christian believers and in the Christian communities of which they are members. These various authors all write within a common viewpoint with regard to the work of the Spirit; as each is addressing a different pastoral situation, each draws attention to different elements in the Spirit's work and has his own particular emphasis.

When we turn to the elements of diversity in the treatment of the Spirit's work by the New Testament authors, the use of the term Paraclete, solely in the Johannine writings, is a very obvious example of particular usage. In our final chapter we shall draw some attention to this feature in the tradition and to the theme suggested by it, namely that the Spirit is our counsel, both prosecuting and defending.

It is not surprising that the Lukan writings have been so influential on subsequent Christian thinking about the Spirit; Luke's gospel contains many references to the Spirit in connection with the conception and birth of Jesus as well as with his ministry, and the Acts extends the period surveyed to include the first three decades of the Christian Church, with the implicit understanding that the era of the Church will continue for a long time. This presentation has governed the evolution of the Christian year; it has also influenced the phraseology of familiar prayers, of blessings, and even of the baptismal questions which might be taken to imply that God worked in successive phases as Father in creation, as Son during a brief period for our salvation, and now in the era of the Church as Spirit for our sanctification. According to this linear view of revelation the Spirit unfolds and communicates to us what has already been achieved by the Son. As we have seen, this treatment of the saving history is consistent with the view that the era of the Spirit opened with Pentecost and the Spirit's principal sphere of operation is the Christian Church.

We do not in any way deny or contest that the Holy Spirit is particularly at work in the Church by covenant and promise, and that participation in the Spirit within the Church has been a means of growth in holiness for countless Christian believers. Indeed we devote an entire chapter 'Spirit, Sacraments and Structures' to developing some of the implications of these convictions. However, we are not content with the linear model as the most satisfactory one available. It can convey a misleading impression, namely that God worked *successively* either through three different modes of revelation or through three different modes of being. Christian writers, both within the patristic period and more recently, have drawn on the wide range of biblical material, to which we have already made some reference, and tried to relate the various biblical insights and assertions with the fundamental Christian belief that God is Trinity. The linear view on which we have already touched led naturally to an understanding of the godhead closely linked with the work of God in creation and salvation, with the divine 'economy' as it has sometimes been called. However, in no sense did God *become* Trinity; God is and always has been Trinity. Once that point has become clear, it follows that in whatever one Person of the Trinity does the others always and necessarily have their part to play, and that all are fully involved in creation, redemption and sanctification. (As we have already noted, this will be treated more fully towards the end of the next chapter). We have taken this fundamental tenet of the faith with full seriousness, and it has affected our thinking in three principal respects.

First, with regard to our own experience of the Christian life we have explored the implications of Paul's thinking, particularly in Romans 8. Through the agency of the Spirit believers are caught up, as it were, into the life of the Godhead, incorporated through the activity of the Spirit into the Son, given there the firm and assured status of children of God by adoption, enabled to join in the Son's ceaseless prayer of *Abba* to the Father. This chapter in the Epistle to the Romans presents to us the being and work of God as irreducibly and necessarily threefold rather than monist or bipolar; the experience of Christian praying provides a corroboration of this insight and a foretaste of that communion or fellowship of the Holy Spirit, in whom we have fellowship with the Father and with his Son Jesus Christ. An important consequence of this understanding of the being and work of the Spirit is the seriousness and depth which it perceives in prayer and worship. Prayer, both individual and corporate, is the means whereby we through the Spirit are enabled, as it were, to share in and grow in the divine conversation of love, both initiative and response, which constitutes the relationship of Father and Son. The modern pastel drawing reproduced on the cover of our report attempts to express this visually.

Second, if God be Trinity, then the Spirit works together with the Father and the Word in the work of creation. A purely biblical theology may not at first sight lead us to that conclusion, but any attempt at systematic theology which takes trinitarian faith seriously must do so, and in so doing it will pick up and develop hints in the biblical tradition. Thus a chapter entitled 'The Holy Spirit and Creation' is an integral part of our work; in it we have sought to do justice to fundamental trinitarian insights in terms which are consistent both with the biblical tradition and with our understanding of the world. In this chapter we have drawn attention to the twin elements of order and flexibility, of structure and development, of consistency and openness, of regularity and originality, all of which physical scientists perceive to be at work in the evolving universe. We have sought to show that these elements cohere with biblical conviction that, in the work of God and therefore of the Spirit, we find both order and rationality and also innovation and surprise. In his book *The Holy Spirit* Professor C.F.D. Moule puts forward the argument that generally in the New Testament 'Spirit is confined to the Church and the new creation. Christ has cosmic functions ... but not the Spirit' (p.20). After some further discussion he continues, 'All this is not to say that it is illegitimate to use the term "Spirit" in the broad and generalised way that is now common – provided the user knows what he is doing' (p.21). In our treatment of the work of the Spirit in creation and in the evolving universe we have avoided using the term 'Spirit' in a broad and generalised way, seeking rather to do justice to the implications of a fully trinitarian faith. Moreover, as we have already noted, we are aware what we are doing in building on and developing the explicit biblical assertions about the Spirit's work.

In the same paragraph Professor Moule continues, 'It is extremely difficult to avoid using "inspiration" (which is a "spirit" word) to describe the genius of creative artistry' (p.21). This is one of several factors which have moved us to include in our work a chapter on 'The Spirit and Creativity'. If the work of the Holy Spirit is to be discerned within God's creative activity, then the work of the artist and craftsman, of the inventor and researcher are spheres in which we should properly expect to find the Holy Spirit at work. This chapter refers especially to the work of the composer, the painter, the poet and the novelist; in the work of them all there is an element of imaginative engagement with the constraints of certain forms and means of expression, a combination not unlike that which we discerned in the way in which God is continuously active in creation. Since we are created in God's image, it is appropriate to think of human creativity as a reflection of God's own creativity.

The third important implication of our fundamental conviction about the trinitarian nature of the being of God lies in our conviction that the Spirit, though particularly at work within the Christian Church (as we have noted) by covenant and promise, is also at work outside it, in the lives and characters of people of other faiths and of no faith. We touch on this point in our chapters concerning creation and creativity. Indeed at several points in this book we note in passing that the Spirit is active outside as well as inside the Christian Church, for 'the wind blows where it wills' (John 3.8). The same Greek word means both *wind* and *spirit*. This point coheres naturally with the other two, both of which tried to do justice to the presence and activity of God (and *a fortiori* of the Holy Spirit) outside the confines of the Church. Naturally the touchstone of the quality of the Spirit's activity in the life of any person, whether Christian or not, is the evidence of a Christ-like spirit. Wherever that spirit is to be found, it must surely be attributed to the unseen, inward working of the Holy Spirit. A haunting chant often sung in our churches and popularized by the Community of Taizé contains the words, 'Ubi caritas et amor, Deus ibi est' (Where there is love and charity, there is God), and if God be there, then the Holy Spirit must be there, for the Spirit is pre-eminently the Spirit of love; more still, the Spirit is believed to be the very Spirit of love who binds together Father and Son in their reciprocal self-giving.

Our conviction that the Holy Spirit, while particularly at work within the Church, is also at work outside led us to consider carefully the possibility of our devoting more attention, in connection with this report, to the Spirit's work in relation to other faiths. We came to the conclusion that other faiths are more appropriately discussed under the heading of Salvation, itself the subject of our next report. Having merely mentioned here this important dimension of our subject, we intend to return to it for more thorough treatment in our next report.

The principle set out just now in connection with the first two consequences of taking trinitarian faith seriously, namely that rationality and inspiration are not incompatible with one another and indeed require one another, has informed our understanding of the work of the Spirit in connection with the charismatic revival. Another way of expressing this principle is to say that God is a God of order as well as of freedom, of continuity as well as of innovation, of regularity as well as of surprise. If all this is true about God, it must hold true of the Holy Spirit. That we understand to be the overriding message of 1 Cor. 12-14, an extended passage which bears directly on problems attending manifestations of the Spirit in the Corinthian church. There is no doubt that in our day the charismatic movement has brought spiritual vitality to many individuals and congregations and thus to the life of the Church as a whole. However, all religious movements, and indeed religion itself, stand under judgement; all can become subject to rigidity and formality; all types of piety can become means of self-indulgence, and all need to be set repeatedly against the touchstone of Christ-likeness, which is the only authentic mark of the Spirit's activity.

There are indeed varieties of gifts; we value the charismatic movement for all the undoubted good it has brought to the

Church. We make sympathetic response to it and a theological appraisal of some of its features, particularly in our chapter 'Is this that?'. Equally, we wish to affirm and support those whose experience of the Christian life, with regard both to faith and to prayer, has been rather different. For instance, within the principles on which we have worked there is room for regarding rational reflection, which seeks the coherence of all truth, to be just as much evidence of the work of the Spirit as sudden illumination or revelation, for the Spirit is the Spirit of order as well as of surprise. (This is one of the lines of thought developed in our chapter 'The Spirit of Truth'). Similarly we are convinced that not all prayer has to be charismatic prayer; ordinary, apparently pedestrian prayer (that is to say, the daily prayer of most Christians) should be understood as prayer in the Spirit just as much as more spectacular prayer. Further, liturgical prayer in the office and Eucharist, and prayer which struggles or groans in difficulty and darkness, should be valued as authentic praying in the Spirit just as much as the spontaneous, keenly and vividly experienced prayer of the new convert or of the newly charismatic congregation. Within the body of the Church in which varieties of gifts are distributed, we all need one another, and it may well be that we can all critically appreciate one another and learn from one another. Certainly our hope is that our work will help to integrate thought and feeling, the reflective and the affective, within the life of the Church as a whole and in the lives of its individual members.

People quite frequently speak of some phenomena, particularly those displayed in charismatic circles, as signs of the 'direct' activity of the Holy Spirit. Instead of being known through the indirect means of the ordinary life of the Christian community, its words and acts and structures, the Spirit is encountered with no intermediaries or interpreters. Such a view is easy to understand. From the earliest days of Christian faith, people have identified moments of transition in their lives of prayer when they feel they no longer know God at secondhand but can confirm what they have been told by others out of their own experience (cf. John 4.42). But there are problems in using the language of 'direct' and 'indirect' encounter too simply. It will not do to say that God ordinarily acts through indirect means and then for specially important occasions dispenses with them: this would make the incarnation rather hard to understand – as if God could have found a better means of communication than the truly human life and acts and death of Jesus. There is also the danger of imagining that words or insights associated with 'direct' encounter are not subject to the ordinary processes of discernment, reflection and testing in the Christian community. Even in circumstances where we are confident of having broken through some kind of barrier in our relationship with God, we are still the people we always were, our minds and imaginations working in the ways our past experience has made possible for us. God seems never to work by completely annihilating our nature and our history. So perhaps it is better to avoid the problematic language of 'direct' and 'indirect' (or 'immediate' and 'mediated', in the language of Roman Catholic controversies on this question in the '20s and '30s). If we need to signal the significance of the moments of breakthrough and transition, much of the literature on prayer suggests that we should talk of it as a process whereby more and deeper levels of the human personality are brought into our knowing of God, rather than as God acting more directly. It is true that as more of the personality becomes involved, many words or pictures that were once helpful will naturally fall away, and there will be less sense of *consciously* depending on things learned from others. But this should not be taken to mean that at such moments God suspends our human ways of knowing and gives us a kind of other-worldly infallibility. Thus in this book we shall speak a great deal about 'experience of the Holy Spirit', but this should not imply some kind of raw experience independent of the normal functioning of our human powers of understanding and interpretation in the light of tradition.

This introductory chapter has sought to set out some features lying in the background which have led to our choice of this subject; to draw attention to some of the more important convictions which have influenced our own thinking and which we have tried to convey; to indicate the chapters in the report in which these convictions receive fuller treatment. It will be apparent to the reader that we stand in that Anglican tradition of which Hooker is the most celebrated exponent. Thus scripture is our supreme authority; scripture is properly understood within the Church. On questions to which scripture does not address itself the Church may develop the teaching of scripture, so long as it does not contradict scripture. As we noted at the outset, we have not attempted an exhaustive survey of topics associated with the Holy Spirit. It will, however, have become clear that we are persuaded that understanding of the Spirit, knowledge of the world, and engagement in prayer and worship go hand in hand. Therefore it is fitting that the next chapter should be entitled 'Charismatic Experience: Praying "In The Spirit"'; it has been based on a number of interviews with Anglican charismatics in a particular congregation. We were asked to reflect on the charismatic movements; therefore we have gone there first and done some fieldwork, on which we have done some theological reflection.

2

Charismatic Experience: Praying 'In the Spirit'

There is little to attract the unbeliever in the traditional, organized church... We have neglected our prayer life; we have stopped listening to God;... (yet people are) hungry and thirsty for God or or some form of spiritual reality.

(David Watson, 1980)

If the Holy Spirit is in you, you will comprehend well enough His action within you... All those who have been baptized in the Holy Spirit have put on Christ completely; they are children of light and walk in the light which has no decline.

(Symeon The New Theologian, early eleventh century)

The charismatic renewal today calls as controversially as did Symeon in his very different Byzantine milieu for an intense commitment to prayer and the expectation of specific experiential effects from the invocation of the Holy Spirit. Symeon too spoke to what he regarded as a tepid generation in the Church; and for him the blasphemy against the Holy Spirit was precisely the denial that the Spirit could be vibrantly experienced now, 'divinizing' Christians (to use his eastern terminology), catching them up into the very life of the Godhead, making them nothing less than 'sons of God by adoption and grace'. (See Symeon The New Theologian, *The Discourses*, esp. XXIV, 4).

In a similar way that challenge has been laid at the door of the established churches and denominations in the last quarter century by the influx of charismatic influence. And so some hard questions, with which this chapter is concerned, are

17

rightly pressed: *are* we truly a praying Church? What (if anything) do we expect of the activity of the Holy Spirit in prayer? Is the Holy Spirit uniformly and universally present or only sporadically available? Is indeed a failure to reflect on the Spirit any sign of the Spirit's absence (or vice versa)? Does the Holy Spirit always guarantee consoling or emotionally satisfying experiences (as the somewhat misleading translation of Paraclete as 'comforter' could suggest)? And, even more fundamentally, what *is* an 'experience' of the Holy Spirit? Is it in any clear way distinguishable from an 'experience' of the Father or the Son? And, if not, why should we wish to speak of the Spirit as a distinct Person at all?

If we are to confront these issues cogently for today, we must surely do so not just by drawing on scriptural and credal authority (although these are fundamental, as we shall see in the course of this book), but by reference precisely to some of the various and rich experiences of the charismatic constituency in the Church as we find it now. Thus this chapter is largely based on a number of in-depth interviews with Anglican charismatics from a particular church which was deemed to be representative of the development of the movement within the Church of England. The interviews were conducted with men and women of different ages, social backgrounds and education, all of whom have, however, been involved in 'renewal' for some lengthy period (between ten and twenty-five years). They can thus speak with some perspective of time on the phases of development that the movement has undergone in relation to 'prayer in the Spirit', and this at a moment when, self-confessedly, the movement within Anglicanism seems to be facing a crisis of decision and direction which is closely (and interestingly) related to attitudes to prayer. Thus, out of the evidence of contemporary *reportage* emerge theological themes of recurring significance.

The movement within denominational Christianity in general has been said to be in decline: whether this is so in numerical terms is not our concern here, but rather what shifts in understanding may be occurring in relation to our questions about the Spirit and prayer. As a means of comparison in these investigations interviews were also taped with some members of a recent split-off group from the Anglican charismatic church studied, a Fellowship loosely associated with the 'Restoration' movement and now fast making new converts of its own. The members of this group tend to be younger Christians (not necessarily younger in age); they also span an interesting range of class and educational backgrounds: there are professional people here too, and a large gathering of students, but in general the ethos is less middle class than in the Anglican congregation. Manifesting a much purer 'sect'-like form than can be achieved within the episcopal structures of Anglicanism, and also a much more rigorous biblical fundamentalism, this group's maintenance of high levels of prophecy and public tongue-speaking in its worship distinguishes it from what is now the norm in its present Anglican counterpart. Here worship had already become somewhat formalized and sedate before the split-off, and indeed for those who left this was seen as a loss of contact with the Spirit's drive and purpose. The Anglicans have in the meantime reverted to at least the outlines of the ASB's requirements.

Is this a sign of decline and lack of direction in the Anglicans' case (as the Fellowship tends to read it), or rather a new phase of deepening maturity, a distinct pressure of the Spirit towards a new synthesis with tradition (as the Anglican minister reads it)? To answer this, we need to look at the witness of those concerned, and only from there suggest a theological judgement based upon this. What is sure, however, is that we have here a fascinating correlation of sociological and theological factors, different attitudes to the Holy Spirit and prayer being *aligned* with different socially-constituted groupings. To anticipate: the purer 'sect' form, with its rejection of ordained ministry, commitment to egalitarian exercise of 'gifts' (and yet strict refusal of teaching roles to women on fundamentalist grounds), expects high feeling states as the norm in public prayer 'in the Spirit'; whereas the Anglican community, with its self-styled hybrid of 'sect' and 'church'-type organization (the episcopal structure combined with 'elders' and much lay leadership, including some cautious use of women in positions of authority), seems to be moving towards a less sporadic and emotionally dramatic understanding of the Spirit, encouraged by its minister to believe that a new phase of the renewal has been entered, the 'recovery of gifts' being succeeded by the 'recovery of disciplines'. How does this shift of emphasis affect the theological questions with which we are concerned? And what broader theological and historical perspectives may we apply to the divergence between the two groups? We shall look at a number of selected questions in turn.

1. ENCOUNTERING RENEWAL, 'EXPERIENCING' THE SPIRIT

(a) The Interviews

It was in questions concerning the initial 'experience' of the Spirit, and the continuing effects of regular prayer 'in the Spirit', that we found least divergence, indeed, negligible divergence, between the two groups. The vexed question of the meaning of 'baptism in the Spirit' (addressed in detail in the next chapter) was not explicitly raised by the interviewer, and, perhaps significantly, was not an issue for polemicizing by either group. But to the general question, 'How has your prayer changed since you encountered renewal?', there were answers such as, 'There was a sense of new *excitement*', or, 'It was so delightful to find that it was acceptable to be openly *enthusiastic* about God'. 'Affective' (positive emotional) states, then, were universally acknowledged, the sense of a great release of feelings, especially positive feelings of praise and exaltation, that had previously been held back. But even more significant for our question about what characterizes the 'experience' of the Spirit, specifically, was the reiterated remark that people had in a new way found prayer to be a 'two-way

20

relationship', not just a talking at God, but God (the Holy Spirit) already co-operating in one's prayer, energizing it from within, and no less also responding in it, alluring one again, inviting one into a continuing adventure. This was said to be 'the real thing', 'making yourself a channel for the Spirit's work', an intermingling of the human desire for God and the Spirit's interceding to the Father (cf.Rom. 8.27). With this then came the sense of prayer in the Spirit becoming a uniting thread in one's life, 'an all-encompassing relationship', so that prayer became no longer one activity (or duty) amongst others, but the wellspring of all activities. Thus Paul's injunction 'Pray constantly' (1 Thess. 5.17) took on a new meaning, as did Jesus' insistence on trust, faith, and confidence in prayer ('Ask, and it will be given you' (Matt. 7.7)), even though it was admitted that one did not always get what one expected.

(b) Commentary

The actual prayer methods of the people interviewed were enormously varied, as varied as were the people themselves. It was taken for granted that there would be a commitment (indeed an intense commitment) to the usual range of verbal prayers, expressing penitence, praise, petition and intercession; but beyond that most people also made regular and disciplined use of some sort of scriptural meditation. Moreover, it was striking how ingenious and resourceful people had been in working out structured patterns of praying suitable for their own psychological type or mode of life. One husband and wife were somewhat startled to have the interviewer comment that their preferred methods of prayer were almost indistinguishable from (respectively) Luther's 'Simple way to pray' (using each phrase of the Lord's Prayer meditatively in turn), and Ignatius Loyola's 'composition of place' in *The Spiritual Exercises* (thinking one's way imaginatively into a gospel scene). Being of a fundamentalist bent they preferred not to rely on 'tradition', but had painstakingly evolved their own ways.

Likewise, it is worthy of comment that the expected reference to Romans 8.14-27 (in relation to the crucial experience of the Spirit praying in one) did not in general lead to any clear reflection on the importance of this in *trinitarian* terms. The interviewees assumed without question that the Spirit was in some almost inexplicable way experientially distinct from the Son (despite the confusing shifts in Paul's language in Romans 8.9f.). But the possibility that this experiential starting point might provide some sort of response to those theologians currently challenging the Spirit's distinct personal existence, or otherwise dismantling the doctrine of the Trinity, was far from their minds. In general these controversies had not impinged on them at all (as indeed would be true in most parish contexts). Distant too was any thought that ontological trinitarian reflection might be 'earthed' here, leading perhaps to a reassimilation of the eastern patristic model of 'deification' with which Symeon was familiar – the Spirit *incorporating* one into the life of sonship and so bringing one to the Father.[1] Such categories sounded alien to those of fundamentalist background, although there was a marked, and perhaps unexpected, willingness to consider the possibilities. In short, and doubtless unsurprisingly, there was little knowledge shown of trinitarian controversies in Christian tradition at all, or of where in the history of east/west divergence on this issue the charismatic approach would find its natural allies, if any.

That this is unsurprising, moreover, is a matter in part of our western religious heritage, with its much bemoaned bifurcation of thought and feeling, scholastic theology and piety; and this historical background is worthy of brief (if inevitably over-simplistic) reflection, especially in view of charismatics' much-vaunted claims to a recovery of spiritual 'wholeness'. For not long after Symeon was controversially reasserting the significance of the felt apprehension of the Spirit in the east,

---

[1] This approach was pursued systematically in *We Believe in God*, chapter 7, and is vividly expressed in our cover picture.

the west too, though in very different cultural and political circumstances was engaged in an extraordinary shift of consciousness which also evidenced a fresh discovery of 'feeling'. The twelfth century, it has been argued, produced the 'discovery of the individual'; it also witnessed the rise of the age of chivalry, and the complex rituals of courtly love. In the Church's musical life of late twelfth-century France, too, were unleashed strikingly passionate ululations, elongated melismas wound over the traditional plainsong chants. The theological counterpart of all this, one might argue, was Bernard of Clairvaux's fresh assimilation of affective strands in Augustine, which resulted in a new turn to 'feeling' as an indispensable component in spiritual growth. 'Instruction makes us learned', says Bernard, 'but feeling makes us wise'. Moreover he could go on to make startling use of erotic imagery in his construal of the soul's desire for God. He was, after all, addressing young monks in the Cistercian reform who had not been shielded from an adolescence in the world by growing up as child oblates.

Yet if writers in the twelfth century moved to incorporate feeling and body metaphors as positive features in spiritual development, by the fourteenth century there was a discernible, and tragic, disjunction occurring between intellectual, scholastic approaches to God on the one hand, and pietistic feeling-and-body-oriented approaches on the other. This was carried over in a different way into theories of prayer, so that, for instance, 'contemplation' could be construed either as the pure 'intellect' communing with God or, quite differently, as a deliberate shutting down of the mind in favour of the will or 'affectivity'. In a variety of ways piety and theology were being rent apart in the west.

Thus it is a striking irony that, in the fourteenth century, just as Gregory Palamas' defence of 'hesychast' practices was defending the use of the body in prayer and effecting in the east an extraordinary and unexpected *synthesis* of 'affective' and 'intellectual' traditions of prayer in that context, the west was busy driving a wedge between them.

Moreover, we are still in thrall to these disjunctions, as the history of western Christian sectarianism since the late medieval period witnesses. For here it has tended to be the sectarians *in revolt* who have highlighted, sometimes in extreme forms, the significance of 'affective' or 'enthusiastic' prayer-states, and simultaneously claimed the (neglected) Holy Spirit as their own. In this western historical perspective, then, the contemporary charismatic movement calls forth a certain feeling of *déjà vu:* the pietistic emphasis on feeling and bodily response, the sectarian ethos, the claims to direct experience of the Spirit, and an undercurrent of strong anti-intellectualism – all these might be expected to hang together in the western context just described. Even if such western movements are not demonstrably a manifestation of social or economic 'deprivation', then, they may bespeak a more subtle form of 'affective' deprivation in 'church' type western Christianity, a deprivation which goes back to the same divide between 'affectivity' and intellect, spiritual experience and reflective tradition, to which we have just drawn attention and which may be characteristic of western (or at least of North Atlantic) culture as a whole.

What is new in contemporary 'renewal', however, and so vital for our present concern of prayer and the Spirit, is the incorporation of this 'sectarian' constellation of themes *within* established 'church' frameworks, including Anglicanism. Could this in fact provide the possibility of a new *rapprochement* between the disjunct traditions which we have been considering: affective piety on the one hand, and informed reflective theology on the other (the latter rooted as much in an intellectual assessment of *tradition* as of the Bible)? That this tension might be ridden is self-confessedly not the aim of the purer 'sectarian' house-churches currently fast gaining adherents. But that it may be the task implicitly confronting intra-Anglican charismatics, in a new phase of their development, is borne out further by reflection on the specific theme of 'tongues'.

2. THE SPIRIT AND 'TONGUES'

(a) Interviews

Here we can indeed chart a distinct difference of emphasis between the two groups studied. For whereas the Anglican charismatics in the church have now almost ceased to use tongues in public worship (the exception being the occasional, unplanned, and indeed eerily beautiful use of corporate 'singing in tongues'), the Fellowship group deliberately encourages corporate praise in tongues, especially in the often jubilant and noisy introduction to their services, and claims a much greater 'cutting-edge' and 'specificity', too, to their public prophecies. The divergence may partly result from the departure of some of the more 'activist' worshippers from the one group to the other. But there is also, implicitly, a different reading of 1 Cor.14 in play in the two groups. The Anglicans, curbed in public tongue-speaking to some extent by their minister, after some episodes which were thought to be excessive and unedifying, are now preferring in the main to keep their tongue-speaking as a private 'love-language' *to* God (see v.2), having found a plethora of tongues and interpretation somewhat repetitive or trite (see v.19). In contrast the Fellowship is much more anxious to exhibit the 'gifts' in their full range (especially tongues and prophecy, understood as sent *from* God), and to witness to 'unbelievers' and potential converts (vv.21ff.). Here, then, is a noticeable difference in opinion over whether the Spirit's presence always is, or should be, publicly or dramatically manifest.

But in fact it is in the private use of tongues that the most interesting material emerged in discussion with the Anglicans. For it was striking, again, how in certain ways their (very diverse) use of tongues converged spontaneously on certain themes from the contemplative traditions of the Church, traditions with which most of them were not in any direct way familiar, and indeed against which their fundamentalist convictions would naturally prejudice them. Thus, whereas the dominical warning against 'vain repetitions' (Matt. 6.7 AV made them wary of repetitive or mantric prayer, even of the 'Jesus prayer', they were ready to acknowledge that their 'tongues' often had a repetitive and formalized sound, and could be serving a similar function. Some, indeed, used 'tongues' as a regular discipline of prayer. A memorable example was a charismatic plumber, who often prayed in tongues as he worked alone. ('There are some very prayerfully laid pipes in this area', he remarked).

Similarly, whereas some saw silence in prayer as mainly an absence of thought, or a sign of perplexity, and wished to *fill* such silence with tongues, others could voice the thought that silence could actually be the 'point' or 'end' of tongues, that to which tongues naturally led. (Certainly this could sometimes be witnessed communally in a very sensitive and quiet use of 'singing in tongues' at the evening service, ebbing away into intense stillness and corporate awareness). Thus, when faced with the charge of the Fellowship group that the Anglicans were losing their 'cutting-edge' in playing down their public use of tongues and prophecy, the minister's response was, 'God is trying to speak to us: *that* should be the feeling.' Others said there had been a certain 'hardness' in some of the more strident public tongues, which had simply 'felt wrong'.

It was the diversity of the application and theological interpretations of private tongues that was most remarkable, however. It was said to be a 'short cut' to God, a direct release of joy or feeling, a way of 'getting out of the way' so that the Spirit could act directly, a prayer for when 'words failed', whether through loss, perplexity or grief, a means of becoming 'like a child' (see Matt. 18.3), or, used authoritatively, a prayer for warding off danger. While only a few interviewees were familiar with, or happy with, the psychological language of 'releasing the unconscious', or 'exposing one's inner life' to God, all stressed the healing qualities of this prayer, its directness, and its short-circuiting of normal checks and defences. Above all the theme of 'ceding to the Spirit' was stressed, the way in which tongues averted one's normal and natural tendency to 'set the agenda', especially in the areas of counselling and illness. Tongues were found to reach directly to the root of a problem, so that 'if one did not know what to pray for before, one does afterwards' (see Rom. 8.26). In sum, it was found in the Anglican community that tongues were continuing to be used in diverse and rich ways, in private prayer, in small house groups, and in the semi-private counselling or healing sessions which attended evening communion. But more overt or spectacular usages of tongues in public contexts had become the prerogative of the Fellowship group.

(b) Commentary

The Anglicans, with almost no exception, were emphatic that tongues were 'not the be all and end all', although they admitted they might not have said that a decade ago. They felt that this gift had 'fallen into place', and it was not necessarily for everyone; whereas in the Fellowship it was expected as 'normal' for all 'real Christians', and seemed to be being used in a much more overt and self-conscious way as an (effective) instrument of conversion alongside the other 'gifts'. Only a few interviewees, however, knew anything of the instances of 'tongue-speaking' found in spiritual writers dotted through the tradition. Interestingly here, in writers as contextually diverse as the Desert Fathers and St Teresa, what is noteworthy is how little is made of it: it is simply a natural outflowing of expressiveness in one already deeply committed to prayer. It is recorded of abba Ephraim, for instance, that his prayer was sometimes like 'a well bubbling out of his mouth' (*Apophthegmata Patrum,* Ephraim 2). Over a thousand years later Teresa's autobiography quite passingly refers to a type of

prayer in which 'The soul longs to pour out words of praise...
Many words are then spoken... But they are disorderly' (*Life*,
ch. 16). And there are many other such scattered examples
from the tradition, giving the lie to the suspicion that this gift
has been totally dormant since the apostolic age. 'Singing in
jubilation', likewise, is seen by Augustine and others as a
wholly natural way of letting the Spirit pray in one: for 'this
kind of singing *(jubilum)* is a sound which means that the heart
is giving birth to something it cannot speak of' (*Sermons on the
Psalms,* 32.8).

But again, as we have already intimated, only a few interviewees were beginning to take note of the parallelism in
charismatic and contemplative traditions, or to explore the
burgeoning popular literature on this theme of the 'recovery
of disciplines' from such traditions, although this was clearly
being encouraged by the Anglican minister. Once again one
felt that the church was at a point of decision: whether to
modify its exclusive biblicism, accept a quieter form of worship, and turn to a broader and more intellectual assimilation
of tradition; or whether to reassert the more overtly 'enthusiastic' worship of some years previously, and engage consciously in 'power evangelism'. A small minority wanted
much more public tongue-speaking to re-emerge (and it is
significant that a few of these people left the church during the
period of this research); others saw its dangers as 'an excuse
not to think' (see 1 Cor. 14.19). Exactly, however, at the axis
of this decision also lie the issues in our last set of themes.

3. PRAYER AND FAILURE, PRAYER AND
ARIDITY, PRAYER AND DEPRESSION

(a) Interviews

It was in these areas that the greatest ambivalence was found
in the interviews, and the ambivalence cut across the two
groups. Does 'failure' in prayer, or the common states of dryness ('aridity') and depression when afflicting those who pray,

indicate that the Spirit is necessarily inactive or impeded here? Is the Spirit's work in any sense compatible with human failure and weakness?

'Failure' in prayer was confronted movingly in one interview with an Anglican 'elder', a man who for long years had wanted to 'come into tongues'. Repeatedly his friends had prayed for this, but to no avail. The same man's wife was also virtually crippled by back pain; again, repeated prayer had brought little relief. It was poignant to have to ask how he could explain this. His response was that he could only finally 'bow to God's sovereignty'; and in relation to tongues, after great disappointment, he had come to accept, 'I've just got to be me, and that's the Lord's job'. When the interviewer enquired whether such evident humility could not itself be a work of the Spirit, he assented, though there was a sense that this was a new idea. One might juxtapose the thoughts recorded by John Cassian here: 'Wonders and powers are not always necessary, for some are harmful and are not granted to everyone... Humility is the queen of all the virtues' (*Conferences,* 15.7).

Attitudes to aridity in prayer were mixed, too. Many of those interviewed felt that joyousness should be the norm (and in the case of one member of the Fellowship group, this was particularly emphatically expressed); but all when pressed admitted to phases of dryness themselves, most explaining them as correlated to stress or other passing human factors. Only one person, interestingly, surmised that dryness might actually be in some circumstances a sign of progress, of the Spirit 'driving one into the desert' to 'sharpen one's thirst' (see Mark 1.12f.). But no sustained explanation of this was made; there was no reference, for instance, to St John of the Cross' detailed explication of this as the prayer of 'the night of sense', moving one on into 'contemplation', a form of prayer emotionally less satisfying than before, even felt as a 'failure' to pray, and yet characterized by a continuing and restless desire for God.

On depression, however, there was the widest range of response. A minority of people (in both the Fellowship and the Anglican church) felt that depression was largely self-absorption and should be dealt with rapidly and effectively by prayer and exhortation. People in both groups believed in the devil and the demonic but on the whole were not happy with the idea that individual demons caused illness or depression (a view powerfully influential in the area, however, as a result of the 'demonic deliverance' liturgies of a 'healing centre' recently established locally). This sort of particularized personification of evil had been deliberately averted by the minister within the Anglican group. In a particularly interesting interview with a psychiatrist, who is also a member of the Anglican congregation, it was admitted that being a Christian was sometimes a distinct 'risk factor' in depression, because of the possible mood swings from a high affective state into the reverse, the rigorous standards imposed upon the self, and the feelings of further guilt if prayer was not effective in relieving the condition. Often she found the best way through was to set aside theological language altogether, and insist, 'This *isn't* a sin problem; you have a health problem that can be effectively treated with drugs.' It was important, then, that religious people should feel no guilt or shame about accepting medication when needed. The same doctor was, however, wary of saying that the Spirit could in any way be working actively in and through a depression, especially severe psychotic states, although she conceded that 'less severe episodes' could sometimes lead to a 'greater dependence on God'.

In general, then, there was an agreement amongst those interviewed that Christians should not normally be depressed, and that their mood should primarily be characterized by joy. Once again there was only one commentator who strongly urged that to demand the continuous maintenance of a high feeling state was actually 'unbiblical'. 'What of Gethsemane, not to speak of the prophets and the psalms?' The same person distinguished importantly between clinical 'depression' and spiritual 'desolation'. The former he saw as a recognized 'illness', and, just as Jesus had in the gospel stories invariably responded to those who requested healing from sickness, so in this case, too, he believed, the sufferer should rightfully pray to be relieved. In the case of spiritual 'desolation', however, (and he admitted depression and desolation might be difficult to disentangle without the discernment of an experienced spiritual guide), one could be confronting the particular activity of the Spirit itself, moving one on into a painful new phase of growth, a sharing in some sense in Christ's own passion.

(b) Commentary

It was clear that here we had reached a theological crux. If the Spirit's activity was deemed in some sense incompatible with 'low' feeling states, then either a necessarily sporadic understanding of the Spirit's activity was in play, or else there was a lurking dualism (as in the questionably orthodox early fifth-century Macarian homilies, where Satan and the Spirit wage war with equal force for the overlordship of the 'heart', the Spirit being associated particularly with the 'feeling of assurance'). But what then of the possibility of genuinely Christ-like dereliction? Could it not be, as von Balthasar has so movingly expressed it in his theology of 'Holy Saturday', that the Spirit may not only on occasion drive one into a sharing of Christ's desolation, but actually be that in God which spans the unimaginable gulf between despair and victory?[1]

Such thoughts about the Spirit are already foreshadowed in the New Testament (e.g. Rom. 8.11,17). But they have been spelled out since then with the profoundest practical and psychological insight by spiritual writers as diverse as

---

[1]See Plate 3, where Blake's reinterpretation of this classical western 'throne of grace' (see Plate 1) seems visually to anticipate something of von Balthasar's theme.

Diadochus of Photice in the east (fifth century) and John of
the Cross in the west (sixteenth century). Diadochus, for
whom 'regeneration' in the Spirit is central, speaks of God
deliberately 'receding' at times 'in order to educate us', 'to
humble the soul's tendency to vanity and self-glory'; through
'feeling ourselves abandoned ... we become more humble and
submit to the glory of God' (*One Hundred Texts,* 89, 69). This
is somewhat akin to John of the Cross' first 'night of sense',
where prayer seems to lose all its former sweetness. Much
more terrible, though, is John's description of the trials and
disorientations of the second 'night of spirit', in which God
draws so painfully and purgatively *close* that the experience is
akin to that of a log being thrown into a devouring fire (*Dark
Night,* Bk. II. X). If such as this, then, is truly an implication
of Paul's invitation to be compelled by the Spirit into the sharing of Christ's passion, then it has to be said that it is an implication on which so far only a few of those interviewed in
our survey had reflected deeply.

Here too, then, it may be that the charismatic movement
now faces a dilemma, and one with fundamentally trinitarian
implications: is the Spirit only to be a 'triumphalist' Spirit,
bearer of joy and positive 'feeling'? Or, if this is Christ's
Spirit, breathed out of his scarred body, 'one in being' with
Father and Son, must we not allow as much for the fire of
purgation (Eliot's 'flames of incandescent terror') as for the
refreshment of the comforting dove? William Temple's
memorable words are worthy of recollection here:

> When we pray 'Come, Holy Ghost, our souls inspire', we had
> better know what we are about. He will not carry us to easy
> triumphs and gratifying successes;... He may take us through
> loneliness, desertion by friends, apparent desertion even by God;
> that was the way Christ went to the Father... He may lead us
> from the Mount of Transfiguration (if He ever lets us climb it) to
> the hill that is called the Place of a Skull... The soul that is filled
> with the Spirit must have been purged of all pride or love of ease,
> all self-complacence and self-reliance; but the soul has found the
> only real dignity, the only lasting joy. Come then, Great Spirit,

come. Convict the world; and convict my timid soul.'
(*Readings in St John's Gospel,* 16.8-11, pp.288f.).

CONCLUSION

In this chapter we have confronted recurring issues of prayer
and desire, prayer and feeling, prayer and pain. The material
gleaned from the interviews and participant observation cannot in itself, and without further reflection, solve the hard
questions about the nature of the Spirit posed at the beginning
of the chapter; but just as 'sect' and 'church' diverge in
theology as well as social structure, it is clear that our
Anglican community is caught in that tension, and poised in
the act of decision between vying theological possibilities.
And it may well be, as its minister strongly believes, that it
stands on the brink of new, and deeper, perceptions of the
Spirit's guidance and intent for the future of the charismatic
movement as a whole.

What all the charismatics interviewed shared, however, and
what they continue to challenge the Church with, is a deep
and impressive commitment to the adventure of prayer, and
the call to rediscover an unimpeded participation in that infinite desire of God for God which we call the Spirit, and in
which we are drawn into union with Christ. That it is indeed
possible to enter into this divine relationship with willing and
excited co-operation is what the movement, in all its diversity,
testifies to. But it is a participation that can never allow the
certainty of attainment or superiority: Bernard of Clairvaux
has well said, 'There is no proof of the presence of the Spirit
which is more certain than a desire for ever greater grace' (*2nd
Sermon on St. Andrew,* 4). Indeed, if Bernard is right, we may
well reassure those harbouring anxieties about 'sinning against
the Holy Spirit', that their very disposition of penitence and
concern is an indication of this divine desire in them (see also
below, Chapter 10, 'The Holy Spirit and the Future'). Where
there *is* prayer, then, and above all that inchoate desire for
'ever greater grace' which destroys all complacency, there in-

33

deed is the Spirit already active and effective. Or, as John Chrysostom put it conversely, 'If the Holy Spirit did not exist, we believers would not [even] be able to pray to God' (*Sermons on Pentecost,* 1,4).

In this sense, then (to return to the hard questions we posed at the outset), *all* prayer is prayer 'in the Spirit'[1]; for it is already prompted – however unconsciously in the pray-er – by that divine restlessness that ceaselessly yearns towards the Father. And in this sense, too, a failure to reflect consciously and *theologically* about the Spirit is only a failure if there is also a failure in prayer itself, a failure, that is, to court that flow of divine reciprocity within one, to invite God as Spirit (as Diadochus once put it with a lovely artistic metaphor) to 'paint the divine likeness on the divine image in us' with the 'luminosity of love' (*One Hundred Texts,* 89).

As for our question about the experimental *distinctiveness* of the Spirit in prayer, here is an area where the supposedly remote concerns of early Church trinitarianism are pressingly apposite, and perhaps especially for charismatics. For while charismatics run no danger at all (as others may) of neglecting or relegating the Spirit to metaphysical redundancy, there may be, as we have hinted, a danger of associating particular *sorts* of experience with the Spirit (and possibly others with the Son and Father); and this, as the debates of the fourth century highlighted, may lead either to an implicit tritheism (a belief in three different gods), or else to a sporadic, instrumentalist, and possibly impersonal, vision of the Spirit.

It was precisely to counteract such possibilities that the

---

[1]See again Rom. 8.9ff. for the characteristically Pauline themes of the Spirit's 'indwelling', and of prayer as precisely the prior activity of the Spirit in one. In line too with this generalized interpretation of 'prayer in the Spirit' is Eph. 6.18: 'Pray *at all times* in the Spirit, with all prayer and supplication'. With this theme of the Spirit's omnipresence should be carefully contrasted Paul's phrase in 1 Cor. 14.15: 'I will pray with the spirit', in which Paul is commending the openness to God of the *whole person,* both through the reflective mode of prayer, and through prayer as a more direct response to God ('as I am inspired to pray', NEB).

language of 'one in being' was applied to the Spirit alongside Father and Son. For our experience of the Spirit is an experience of *God*, no less, and whatever divine characteristics are experienced in the Spirit are also the divine characteristics of Father and Son. What then of the *distinctiveness* of the three? Fumbling to express the inexpressible, the late fourth century Cappadocian Fathers spoke (in what seems to us forbiddingly abstract terms) of the 'internal relations' of the three Persons as being their only distinguishing feature. Their attempted explanations were often abstruse and polemical, and assumed a philosophical framework which we no longer take for granted. But fundamentally they argued from their own profound spiritual experience: if the Spirit was that in God which constantly called and provoked them (most explicitly in prayer) in yearning towards the Father, then it was the Son, in his filial dependence on the Father, with whom they were being united through this life of prayer. In other words, it could not be different *sorts* of 'experience' (in the sense of emotional tonality) that were associated with the three Persons in their one divine flow of activity, but only the particular way they were related to one another internally: Father as source of all, Spirit as divine goad in restless quest for creation's return again to the Father, Son as the divine prototype of that redeemed and transformed creation. The Spirit then was *eternally* active, ceaselessly 'indwelling' the 'saints', to use Pauline language; this was not to deny *particular* goadings of the Spirit, too, the divine freedom to direct and prompt in special or dramatic ways, as is more characteristic of the Lukan theology of the New Testament.

But why, one must probe further, did the early Fathers need to call the Spirit a *distinct* Person? In the case of the Son this was obvious: he had been incarnate, had prayed to the Father as clearly distinct from himself. But why should not the Spirit be seen merely as a metaphorical expression for the divine outreach? In the lengthy process of developing a trinitarian theology, was it simply an accident that the Spirit was declared a distinct Person, by a rather simplistic deduction from the threefold structure of the baptismal formula? If we are to understand the real logic of this process of theological evolution and to respond convincingly to the suggestion that we are here dealing only with metaphors, we must continue to explore what it is in the history, language, reflection and experience of the Christian community that has made theology resist such a reduction in the status of the Spirit. And to do this involves, as this chapter has hinted, understanding that area where the experience of charismatics and of contemplatives so significantly converges: in that profound, though often fleeting or obscure, sense of entering in prayer into a 'conversation' *already in play,* a reciprocal divine conversation between Father and Spirit which can finally be reduced neither to divine monologue nor to human self-transcendence. We are dealing here, of course with matters almost inexpressible and thus open to every kind of question about appropriate interpretation. But that there is something irreducible here, which tradition has named 'Spirit', is vividly and freshly testified by the contemporary charismatic movement.

As for the implications of our survey for the relation of the Holy Spirit to 'feelings' – whether pleasurable or painful – this is a matter too, as we have indicated, that calls for deepened trinitarian (and so Christological) reflection, an issue to which we shall return in Chapter 4. But in the meantime we need to look at some more precise exegetical concerns raised also by the charismatic movement. We shall ask whether, and to what degree, the experiences which we claim of the Spirit today can actually be identified within the experiences of the earliest Church of New Testament times.

3

Is this that?

In this chapter we attempt to review that Christian experience
which claims to stand in direct relationship to the reported experience of the first Christians in the New Testament. We do
not provide a survey of the full phenomenology of Christian
experience or spirituality down the centuries, but simply an
evaluation of those present-day affirmations of being inwardly
and sensibly moved by the Holy Spirit. Such claims, to be
worthy of evaluation by the Church, must establish some relationship with the New Testament and to be the fruit of
responsible exegesis of passages from it. In effect, when someone today says 'this' (contemporary experience of the Spirit) is
'that' (apostolic experience of the same Spirit), then we are to
test the claim by the touchstone of scripture.

When we do this, we are perhaps treading old ground, and
yet reading it for contemporary and even novel reasons.
Theologians, particularly those in the reformed tradition, have
generally conceived their task as one of formulating their
theology through a systematic tackling of the scriptures.
There have also been many in past ages (as in the present) who
follow the way of spontaneity, either as the mood of a prophet
has led them, or as they have felt themselves or observed
others to be so moved. It has, however, taken the modern
pentecostalist Christians, and especially their manifestation as
charismatics in the mainline Churches, to lay a great emphasis
upon inner experience, interpreting it as the workings of the
Holy Spirit, whilst referring it to the scriptural revelation.
This moves us to express their doctrine as 'this is that', for
they use the precedent of Peter's address on the day of Pentecost (Acts 2.16), when the phenomena then evident were

interpreted as the fulfilment of earlier scriptures. The formula, 'this is that', sums up a particular genre of exposition. Because it refers itself to scripture, we follow its own principles and test its exegesis.

In the New Testament there are both individual and communal models for the Spirit's operation. The individual model, which predominates in the Old Testament, persists but it is not the norm. Thus the Spirit is believed to operate within the community of faith. Nevertheless individuals can receive the Holy Spirit (e.g. Acts 19.2; Gal. 3.2), be full of the Spirit (e.g. Acts 6.3; 11.24), speak through the Spirit (e.g. Acts 2.4; 21.4). Moreover, those who received the Spirit seem to have received clear evidence in their own lives that the Spirit had come upon them; even if they were not absolutely overwhelmed by the transcendent, their experience seems to have been almost independent of their own selves or wills. They may not have felt better (that would be a hard point to investigate, though one imagines they usually did); yet they did most certainly act differently. The most notable instances of people so receiving the Spirit are in Acts 8 (the Samaritans) and Acts 10 (Cornelius' household).

In the former instance there was something so visible that Simon Magus could ask for the power to imitate the apostles who were, apparently, by their prayer with the laying on of hands bringing the Samaritans to a point of crisis. One most naturally reads the passage in the sense that the apostles passed down the row of disciples; that as they did so, they laid their hands on the disciples; and that, as if a spectacular wave or ripple followed them, the recipients were audibly or visibly affected in word or tone or deed. Why else should Simon Magus have thought there was something worth purchasing?

In the latter instance, that of Cornelius, the Gentile household was so dramatically affected that Peter saw and heard enough to make him gasp, 'Quick, get the water'. No doubt in the economy of God it had to be spectacular if it was to convince Peter he should baptize Gentiles. It had to precede the end of his sermon, and certainly to precede the baptism.

We cannot but agree something outwardly notable had happened.

It looks on closer inspection as though, in various other cases of initial conversion reported in the Acts of the Apostles, the first experience of the Spirit is not always so dramatic. Indeed the two instances cited above belong to those dramatic events which mark the crossing of well-signalled boundaries: into the age of the Spirit at the beginning of Acts 2; into Samaria in Acts 8; and to the Gentiles in Acts 10. We gather that the converts in the latter part of Acts 2 are promised the gift of the Spirit (2.38) following repentance and baptism; we also see the beginning of a pattern of joyful, loving and unself-protecting community life. The question at issue is the experience of the Spirit. What then were the disciples experiencing? We may well have a further question: how far may the Church today expect or hope that the conditions of the Spirit's operation in the first generation will be reproduced amongst us? The answer to these questions depends on our establishing what is being reported from the first generation.

Here three notes of caution about the interpretation of scripture need to be made. In the first instance, it is arguable that the Acts and the gospels have been written with a view to establishing some particular patterns of Church life, and particularly that they have been so written for the sake of making some impact on second and third generations of Christians. The case is wide open and in scholarly terms inconclusive. On the other hand, the main Pauline corpus sits immovably in the reigns of Claudius and Nero, and witnesses (however allusively and sometimes infuriatingly) to conditions among Christians of the first generation. But, although Acts portrays Luke as Paul's fellow-traveller, we cannot immediately harmonize passages in the Acts with those in Paul, as if they were all part of one homogeneous literary whole (and perhaps we ought not to want to do so).

Secondly, we recognize that the present Christian experience of the reader may impose a pattern of understanding upon the New Testament text. Just as Peter on the day of

Pentecost said, 'This is that which was prophesied by Joel', so later generations have always been ready to say, 'This is that which was experienced in the New Testament Church'. The apparent force and reality of current Christian experience attaches itself to some part of the New Testament evidence, which becomes to those with the particular experience its non-negotiable point of reference. The pastor and the interpreter of scripture then have the task of affirming, where possible, the integrity and validity of the particular Christian experience, and also of inserting the knife-edge of honest enquiry between that experience and its alleged biblical precedent, archetype or warrant. This is a pastoral task, because such enquiry may well be felt by others as an assault upon their Christian integrity (and indeed on their knowledge of God). Further, to persuade others that this task is proper and Christian, and not ultimately destructive, can liberate the mind in its approach to scripture and also liberate the interior life in the Spirit.

Closely related to this point is the fact that lack of a particular experience among Christian leaders or thinkers at a particular time may also well affect, and indeed govern, their understanding of the New Testament. It can well be argued that because the sixteenth-century Reformers of the Church generally were not experiencing dramatic visitations by the Holy Spirit, they were the more impelled to say 'This is not that', and further (by a kind of spiritual logic), 'We must not expect it to be'. To put this another way: that which was not experienced came to be expounded as unnecessary, or even, in the economy of God, wholly withdrawn or forbidden. Thus there arose in the Reformation period the doctrine that the dramatic visitations of the apostolic age were God's bridging device to bring the Church safely to the period when the whole New Testament would have been written, and at that stage (and only then) 'normal' Church life could proceed. The Reformers were passionately engaged in a battle of ideas and in a struggle for a new approach to the Bible. Those who most prized dramatic Christian experience (the Anabaptists) were observed to be often the most destructive of the existing order. Thus the sixteenth-century Reformers, who wanted everything done 'decently and in order', almost by definition treated the apparent subjectivism of a radical Christian experientialism as incompatible with the goals of the Reformation. The so-called 'phantasizing' of the Anabaptists was strictly beyond the pale, for the Spirit is the Spirit not of chaos, but of order.

With those cautions noted, it is possible to return to the New Testament. What then did the first generation Christians from Pentecost onwards experience? Is it accessible to us? Can it, indeed, be reduced to writing? Does it include outward 'miracle' as well as inward joy and even ecstasy? Further, what status does it have for Christians living today? We may even ask: how far is direct or unmediated experience of Almighty God possible on this earth? In asking this last question we recognize the difficulty of defining what would count as 'direct' and 'indirect'. In our introductory chapter we have already referred to this difficulty, and we note that some at least of the experiences recorded in the New Testament (and it is the New Testament as much as today which is here under investigation) have an immediacy of force about them such as to keep the question before us.

Certain features of the Church's life in the first generation provide a framework for this investigation. The Church was undoubtedly Christocentric. (This Christocentric note occurs repeatedly in this study.) The Lord has risen from the dead, departed from the sight of the first disciples and sent his Spirit. Nevertheless, he was 'with' them always (e.g. Matt. 28.20; John 14 *passim;* Acts 4.29f.). Their faith was directed towards this reigning Jesus, and their service and actions were done in his presence, in his 'Name' (a key concept), and certainly for his sake. Such redirecting of the thrust and goals of human life inevitably affected the feelings, emotions, and moral core of the followers of Jesus, and it was constitutive of the very beginning of Christian experience. We may properly suggest that such experience should be traced to the unseen work of the Spirit, and that the case is not so much psychological as pneumatological. However, the starting point in any reflection by Christians upon their experience would surely have been their response to Jesus, as we have indicated.

Next, we have clear evidence that the Church in its earliest days was undoubtedly a loving fellowship. The free interaction of its members with one another reflected in the early chapters of Acts (and at least sought, if not found, by Paul in his letters) provided an important context for this experience. Supportive and outgoing links of friendship, caring, intimacy, and practical help would themselves be bound to affect this experience. Surely it felt different to be a Christian?

In addition, the Church at its best had a bold front towards society around (e.g. Acts 4.32f.; 1 Cor. 2.4). The necessity (a necessity of both external injunction and internal constraint) for a faithful testimony also surely affected how they felt? At times (e.g. with Stephen) this could lead to suffering. Yet suffering for them was touched with joy and with glory; it was a privilege to suffer for Christ's sake (Matt. 7.13f.; Acts 5.41; Phil. 1.29; 1 Pet. 4.12ff.; etc.), though, even then, some hesitated.

A closely related point is that at some times and places they saw the message of God, the good news, to be powerful in reshaping others' lives and in delivering them into the Christian conviction, the Christian fellowship, and the Christian readiness, if necessary, to suffer for their Lord. The experience of the Church, as it received converts, was bound to be shaped in dependence on the power of this message, power which was understood to be also the power of the Spirit. (The implications of this point are considered at length in Chapter 6).

In association with all these features the following unexpected phenomena are reported in the Acts of the Apostles: extraordinary expressions of thought or feeling ('other tongues'), the 'shaking' of an assembly, highly benevolent providence (e.g. delivery from prison, guidance of route), dramatic healings (including expulsion of demons and raising of the dead), dreams and visions, precognition of the future, and possibly 'prophecy' (though this last may not be extra-ordinary, or it may be included under one or other of the previous headings). On occasion, as in the conversion of Cornelius and his household, several of these phenomena occur in close conjunction and are presented as the means whereby God's goal is achieved. There are also phenomena of judgement, whether temporary (as with Saul's blindness), or more drastic (as with Ananias and Sapphira). Most of these occurrences have parallels in the recorded ministry on earth of Jesus; thus they move the reader towards an integrated understanding of the experience of the first generation of Christians. The principal cause for hesitation arises from the question whether there is (or has to be) a 'this', a present occurrence, genuinely comparable to the 'that' of the New Testament, and, if so, how normative or prevalent such occurrences are in Christian experience. While we need to bear in mind all these features of the Church in its earliest decade, it is clear that the sharpest exegetical question today is raised by the phenomena to which we have just drawn attention. We all may puzzle at the meaning of Jesus' statement that the believer will do greater works than those of Jesus himself (John 14.12) (though this statement may refer to the worldwide ministry of the gospel of salvation and new birth in the name of Jesus); but the specific instances of the actual works of Jesus and their bearing upon the ministry first of the apostles, and second of us, have become for us a major issue in our day.

The modern charismatic movement (at least in Anglicanism) has tended to value very highly the narratives in the Acts of the Apostles, but in practice to depend for its own expectations more upon the gifts listed in various places in the Pauline letters and summarized also in 1 Peter 4.8ff. A common parlance has arisen whereby congregations are characterized as those where the gifts are exercised, and, on inspection, it proves that the common run of such expected gifts is a three-some of tongues, prophecy and healings.

With regard to these gifts, we should note that they are experiences which belong to the whole Church and are given to be shared between Christians. They may, both in theory and in practice, be more moving to the recipients than to the ministrants of the particular gift; in that respect they may be no different from, say, preaching, and but little different from the ministration of sacraments. There is, of course, a practice of speaking in tongues in private prayer, but that is a separate issue, to which we have referred in Chapter 2.

The supernatural feature which has become part of the theological currency of charismatics and does have specific internal implications for the one who has it, is baptism in the Spirit. This is a conventional term for an overwhelming or critical experience of the power and presence of God. Whilst in some circles a claim to this experience might well be interpreted by a non-charismatic as an indication of conversion *de novo,* in more evangelical circles this term is often used to describe a second and post-conversion crisis, not unlike the second blessing of the older holiness movements. It has to be recognized that it is the experience which has led to the use of the terminology. The experience, whilst not received personally by all those who have been labelled charismatics, is nevertheless fairly widespread, and sufficiently so for it to need a common terminology, and to be offered pastorally by the laying on of hands with prayer to those who express their need. It is discussed more fully below.

Scripturally, such a use of the expression 'baptism in the Holy Spirit' has a certain first-blush plausibility: a baptism is a once-for-all event; it has a God-given objectivity; the term can be used metaphorically (as by Jesus about his death); and indeed the teaching of John the Baptist almost suggests that his outward baptism by water is but a shadow of the true baptism which is inward and is the swamping or saturation by the Holy Spirit. However, we need to exercise caution; although the experience of the disciples in the upper room on the day of Pentecost is often expounded as their reception of baptism in the Holy Spirit and as fulfilment of John the Baptist's prediction, there is little other relevant scriptural evidence. There is, however, a passage in which Peter (Acts 11.15f., cf. 15.8) compares the initial experience of the first Gentile converts with the experience of the day of Pentecost. Similar phraseology is used about the phenomena (though without the term 'baptism in the Spirit') in Acts 8 and Acts 19. In the rest of Acts there is no mention of such a baptism, nor is there in the epistles. We have therefore to be careful lest we convert into a universal doctrine of the faith an instantaneous experience which marked three or four special occasions in the Acts of the Apostles, but is not otherwise portrayed as a norm of spirituality or of response to God. These passages encourage us to identify the occasions which are called a baptism as instances of the initial experience of the Holy Spirit, not as a second blessing. This experience, which is often called baptism in the Spirit, should be both welcomed and also tested. It is, however, not universal; true commitment, discipleship, and experience of the Holy Spirit can and do exist without such a crisis. Hence it should not be erected into an essential requirement of the faith, and to call such an experience the baptism in the Spirit can convey the wrong messages, as though it were a norm for every Christian. We may well need for this experience some descriptive term which sounds less like an indispensable requirement and is more in accord with scriptural usage.

If, however, charismatics for the last quarter of a century have been particularly concerned about the three gifts, to which we referred earlier, and about baptism in the Spirit, more recent developments have taken the experiential claims forward into other areas. A notable modern instance is to be found in the ministry of the Californian evangelist, John Wimber. His 'Vineyard' churches both integrate the gospel narratives with the Acts experience and see it as normative for Church life today. The 'Vineyard' exegesis, as generally understood, is typified in an exposition of Matthew 28.20 which interprets the observing of Jesus' commands as truly covering 'all that I have commanded you'. This precludes us from simply referring to it as the obedience to a moral code, as the handing on of a somewhat cerebral gospel, or as the observance of a life of prayer. Rather, the whole scheme of the Church's life, from the Ascension to the Last Judgement, is to be marked unmistakably by those distinctive features of Jesus' own ministry which have a disruptive, miraculous, and yet marvellously salvific character to them. That is how it was in the Acts of the Apostles; indeed Wimber claims that apostolic evangelism is 'power evangelism', the good news reaching people with the miraculous power of God to heal accompanying it. We do not look outside or far ahead for the kingdom; it is with us and within us and among us, and the signs of the kingdom are the clear evidence of it. Signs and wonders, to which we give further attention in our chapter, 'The Spirit and Power', have become more gripping to English charismatics (especially if they have witnessed one of John Wimber's meetings); moreover, the agenda and priorities of Wimber have started to run alongside the older charismatic concerns. Other gifts have come into play also (particularly the 'gift of knowledge'), and a great emphasis has been placed upon Wimber's particular interpretation of the Kingdom. It should be noted that this kind of kingdom theology is the reverse of that of the liberationist, or even of the standard ecumenist; it understands the kingdom to be found within the Church, in narrower compass than the Church itself, whereas in the more usual current exegeses the kingdom lies beyond the Church and has a far wider compass than the Church. Further, in John Wimber's own ministry there has been sufficient evidence of the 'signs following' (cf. Mk. 16.14ff.) for the whole message itself to be widely believed. Whilst this appears to be taking the charismatic emphasis on the 'gifts' in 1 Cor. 12.28 to its logical end, not all charismatics have felt able to follow John Wimber to that end. Indeed we have mentioned the remarkable events associated with John Wimber's ministry without necessarily endorsing their explanation. The facts are well documented; their cause or causes are open to more than one explanation, even to more than one theological explanation.

What then are the new features which are held by some to be a proper part of Christian ministry? Whilst healings are common to older charismatics and the new agenda, the insistence is now that they are the outworking of the programme of signs and wonders. Furthermore, the 'word of knowledge' (1 Cor. 12.8 AV) received a conventional and widely believed exegesis, so that it has come to mean 'divinely given insight into the presence in a room of persons with this or that (nameable) complaint, which God can (or will) heal'. Perhaps each such raising of the contemporary profile of the miraculous has to begin with assertions of the power and goodwill of God towards humanity qualified only by the requirement of faith on the part of the recipients; then, in the light of hard realism and in facing of the facts, the assertions can be subtly qualified. The charismatic movement has had a public life of twenty-five years in the Church of England and has developed sensitivity and self-criticism. John Wimber, however, ranks as a relatively new phenomenon, and he is heard (though he speaks and writes in a fully responsible manner) as reflecting the bolder claims of the earlier phase. There has to be a general readiness to look for God's continuous work (by the Spirit) in the world and in the Church, lest the extraordinary acts of God today appear purely interventionist and seem to testify to God's real absence from the world for the rest of the time, even the surrender of it to the devil.

Before any charismatic movement existed in the mainstream denominations, Lesslie Newbigin was writing in *The Household of God* (1953) that a third strand of authentic Church life was now to be found alongside what he called the institutional model (Catholicism) and the word model (Protestantism), this third strand being the pentecostalist or experiential model, the company of the Spirit. As this strand is now found so strongly within the mainstream Churches, and indeed within the Church of England, its teaching about distinctive features of Christian experience, on which we earlier touched, must inevitably come under scrutiny. We now inspect some of these in turn.

(a) BAPTISM IN THE HOLY SPIRIT

We have already (pp. 44f.) treated this subject quite fully. Here in summary we note our conviction that the pattern discernible in the case of the very first disciples is not to be considered normative for those who become Christians after the outpouring of the Spirit in the upper room at Pentecost; that the arguments for regarding baptism in the Holy Spirit as inseparably linked with conversion and initiation (as set out, for instance, by J.D.G. Dunn in *Baptism in the Holy Spirit*) are compelling; that baptismal language has been inappropriately applied to a later (often dramatic) stage in the Christian life when a believer enters more fully into what he has already received. In short, we are not at all persuaded that the life-changing crisis experienced by not a few Christian people at a time subsequent to their initial conversion is appropriately called baptism in the Holy Spirit. Those who apply this term to this experience need to go to school with the Bible's own teaching on baptism in the Spirit. In the terms of the title of this chapter, we have identified a clear instance in which, in our opinion, 'this' which is experienced to-day is not identical with nor corresponds with 'that' which is alleged to match it in the New Testament.

(b) THE GIFTS OF THE SPIRIT

Three passages from the New Testament particularly claim our attention. In 1 Peter 4. 10f. the gifts may be classified as those of speech and of service to be used in discipleship and in the Christian mission. The list presumably is not exhaustive, but illustrative of a wider principle, namely that individuals with their particular gifts corporately contribute a wide range of faculties, skills and activities.

In Romans 12.6ff. we find a similar pattern, though here we note that some of the gifts appear to be spontaneous or in-stantaneous, whereas others clearly used conscious preparation and planning, and some are of more limited duration than others. Paul underlines the importance of love; each member of the community values the gifts of the others, sees the harmony of the community being promoted by the diversity of its members' gifts, and properly exercises his own gifts as a means of love to others.

We find the most extended treatment of this subject in 1 Corinthians 12. Here the term 'gift' is clearly interchangeable with service or working (forms of work – NEB) (vv. 4ff.). Thus there is no identifiable entity called exclusively a 'gift'. Moreover, the actual functions described in this chapter correspond with the general classification of speech and of service, which we have already discerned with regard to 1 Peter. The 'gifts of healing' (v.9) and 'the working of miracles' (v.10) do, however, raise some further questions about the range of Christian ministering, which we shall shortly consider. However, the principal purpose of this entire chapter in 1 Corinthians is to illustrate the diversity of the body and the divine necessity for its members to live in harmony with one another. Paul could have made his point by any illustration from the variety of functions and gifts within the body. In this chapter he is not intending to concentrate on the particular implications of the various specific activities listed.

We take an illustration from a reference in 1 Cor. 12.8: if anyone today claims, with regard to a gift which he or she is regularly exercising, that 'this' is the 'utterance of wisdom' or 'the utterance of knowledge', the burden of proof must rest with the person who makes the claim. Commentators are by no means clear about the meaning of the expressions used in this passage, and some of the more popular exegesis of this and of other passages appears to be based on an insufficiently careful handling of the text. We thus need to treat with caution any claim to exercise the gifts to which reference is made in 1 Corinthians.

(c) TONGUES AND PROPHECY

In considering these phenomena, which have received much attention in recent years, we turn particularly to 1 Corinthians 14. From time to time we hear charismatic phrases such as, 'This is a church where the gifts of the Spirit are exercised', which means that tongues and prophecy are used in public. Against this background we make the point of detail that (despite the translation in the RSV) the word 'gifts' is not used in 1 Corinthians 14, though it is in 1 Corinthians 12.31. More fundamental is the realization that Paul does not regard tongues and prophecy as the most eminent or most desirable functions. We assume that he was addressing a situation in which prophets and those who spoke with tongues competed with one another and even ceased to worry whether they communicated with one another. Thus Paul invokes the principle that there should be genuine communication between the various members of the Corinthian church, a principle which makes for the edification or building up of the Christian community.

As we consider the ways in which the title of this chapter bears upon prophecy and tongues, we are faced with a particular difficulty. With regard to tongues, are we dealing with unknown sounds which require interpretation, or with unknown sounds which require expression in intelligible speech; or are we dealing with foreign languages known to the speaker and with their translation into a language known to the hearer? It is notoriously difficult to be precisely certain either about the tongues to which reference is made in 1 Corinthians 14 or about the situation in the Corinthian church in terms of which this chapter should be understood. Therefore it is even more difficult to draw from this chapter matters for detailed application in the life of the Church today. We need to learn more about prophecy in New Testament times before we can lightly identify 'this' with 'that'. Moreover, with regard to prophecy also, caution is necessary. In the Old

Testament, and in the early history of the Christian Church as well, there is evidence of both genuine and spurious prophecy. There is a need to test the Spirit and to test the application of any word of God to any particular situation.

It will have been clear from our treatment of tongues and prophecy that we do not consider them to have no proper place in the life of the Church today. Along with a number of other features of the Church's life (e.g. liturgy, prayer, depth counselling, meditation), they can be valuable helps to worship and to the practice of discipleship, but about their derivation from or their revelation in the scriptures we should not assert more than is justified by the evidence. In any case, even if we were certain what tongues and prophecy were in 1 Corinthians 14 and that they were being strongly commended to us in that form, we should need to bear in mind the principles contained in 1 Corinthians 12, that diversity is positively valued and that we are discouraged from desiring the gifts of other people or from insisting that other people should have ours.

(d) HEALINGS

In our chapter 'The Spirit and Power' we give some attention to the healings reported in the gospels and in the Acts of the Apostles. In the epistles they have a place in lists of gifts (1 Cor. 12.9, 28ff.); they are examples of the variety and range of gifts in the Church, but nowhere in the epistles are they treated at length. There is today a great deal of literature about healings and a large corpus of healings actually recorded. Nowadays people may well have different expectations with regard to health from those which were current in New Testament times. Moreover, both then and now healing may properly include the result of the work of doctors. We do not, however, find it easy to make a quick or direct transfer from New Testament times to our own; 'this' and 'that' are not necessarily identical. The Church has certainly been given authority to combat illness, but we do not find evidence in the scriptures to support the view that the Church has been given by its Lord the certainty that the cure of mental or physical illness will always accompany the deeper healing offered.

(e) THE WORD OF KNOWLEDGE

Reference to this gift is made in 1 Cor. 12.8 and nowhere else in the New Testament. This slender basis makes it very difficult for us to determine whether any particular present-day practice or ministry is a 'this' which gives expression to a New Testament 'that'. The explanation of this gift, which we noted on p. 47, may or may not be accurate: namely that it refers to trustworthy insight into the physical complaints of persons whose presence in the room may not even be known. The term is patient of several meanings, and (as with tongues and prophecy) it is exegetically unsound to assert that one meaning which corresponds with some practice in today's Church *must* be for that very reason the one given us by God. Equally, as with other gifts discussed above, any insight into or intuitive understanding of another person's ills should nevertheless be valued highly as a gift from God, even if it cannot be given the title of a scripturally revealed gift of the Holy Spirit.

This discussion of gifts has been restricted to those actually mentioned in 1 Corinthians. We shall not want to tie the notion of gift too tightly nor to limit its range to the specific functions discussed in that epistle. We have concentrated on that epistle in order to meet on their own ground people in today's Church who attribute such importance to the gifts included there. Our own agenda for discussing the experience of the Holy Spirit in today's Church might well concentrate on some rather different gifts and functions.

We conclude our discussion of the gifts claimed by some charismatics with a reference to a very widespread feature of the charismatic movement, namely the sense of joy. This joy is rooted in a keen sense of the nearness of God and in confident conviction of God's immediate engagement with Christian people. As the charismatic movement has matured, so too has this sense of joy; at earlier stages in the movement joy tended to be associated primarily with God's providential care for the individual, now rather more with an awareness of God's sovereignty over the entire world. Further, many people associated with the movement have discovered the integration of joy with suffering to be a crucial stage towards personal and corporate maturity.

CONCLUSION

In this chapter we have been considering and testing some of the claims made by modern charismatics that 'this' which they know at first hand in their own lives and ministries is precisely identical with 'that' which we read in the Acts and in the epistles. We have been maintaining that those who make such claims should test them more thoroughly in the light of the scriptures to which they themselves appeal. That said, 'faithful are the wounds of a friend' (Prov. 27.6). We rejoice that, at a time when there has been a move away from what may have been an excessive concentration on the rational and cerebral in society at large, new joy in the Spirit has deeply affected the life of a somewhat sober institutionalized Church, not least in acting as a counter to a certain type of cerebral and over-verbalized Anglican worship. Put succinctly, the charismatic movement has insistently kept before us certain truths which should have a prominent place in the Christian life: every member of the Church properly has an active ministry; the gospel enables people to be self-accepting, to be transparent to others and to express themselves with openness; there is a dynamic and experiential element in being a Christian; God's power is accordingly to be expected and sought in life and practice, together with a genuinely optimistic hope that God's hand will be at work in the world.

At the same time we feel bound to mention some features of the charismatic movement which have caused pastoral problems, and to make some theological comments on them. In the first place there is a subtle group pressure towards constant joy, with perhaps insufficient awareness of psychological typecasting. The confidence and outgoingness which may be natural to the extrovert (and the insensitive) should not necessarily be viewed as the certain marks of 'victorious living'. The ebullience characteristic of some charismatics may be inappropriate in many lives for internal or external reasons; it may even desert those who have it, when they are under stress, or physical pain, or clinical depression. If the dominant model of Christian daily living and spirituality which those persons encounter is one of continuous euphoria, then the actual Christian fellowship which is supposed to be supportive and therapeutic not only feels uncaring and judgemental to the sufferers, but also inevitably makes any depression worse.

Then we note great prejudice in favour of the inner impulse in the sphere of guidance. The immediacy of God's presence leads believers to expect direct, 'hot line' guidance from God in all, or at least nearly all, situations. This can take various forms: for instance, a prophecy from another which rings true to the recipient's situation, a text of scripture which leaps out and carries a contemporary directive, a dream, an inner urge, a mental picture; all these are recorded, are part of the everyday parlance of charismatics and are open to a friendly critique. However, they need to be tested theologically, both by objective standards of scripture, principles of hermeneutics, and a theology of God's guidance.

Further it is undeniable that in the charismatic movement there is a markedly pietistic strain and there has been a tendency to withdraw from the world and to look inward. The Church of England may well have needed this type of spirituality, and it may well be argued that our society needs this. However, in the last couple of decades Evangelicalism within the Church of England has been recovering a social conscience, which it has integrated with its primary sense of missionary vocation. There are those who regret the extent to which this inward looking strand in the charismatic movement has hindered these developments.

In any case, the charismatic movement sometimes exhibits a frail eccesiology. The doctrine and the institutional life of the Church are frequently downgraded in the movement and regarded as hindrances to the gospel. Earlier in this chapter we touched on the matter of order, which in our chapter on creation we shall develop in a rather different direction. Order is not necessarily boring or trivial, nor is it to be equated with the merely seemly or decorous. Openness to change, vitality, warmth and surprise all need to be balanced by continuity, regularity, stability and rationality. In other words, structure and form are as important as the living content; both should be understood as the work of one and the same Spirit. A similar point is often made with regard to the stress laid within the charismatic movement on certain feelings and emotions as against the proper disciplines of the mind, a matter to which we give further attention in the chapter, 'The Spirit of Truth'.

Under the heading 'Is this that?' we have made an appraisal of some of the claims of the charismatic movement with regard to the present operation of the Holy Spirit. Although we have dwelt on some of the problems raised by the movement, we gladly acknowledge that these problems are mainly the side-effects of a zeal in the Spirit which we wholeheartedly welcome and in which we recognize the hand of God. In this chapter we have been pleading that the distinctive features of that zeal be brought to a more thorough testing in the light of those scriptures to which the movement itself so often appeals. We make this plea for the very reason that we are so deeply appreciative of the movement's strengths. Before we turn to further consideration of the Spirit's work in the Church, particularly in connection with its sacraments and structures, we shall try to do justice to the Christocentric element which has been implicit in our study hitherto, and at times explicit in it.

4

The Spirit of Jesus

The early Christian communities, as we meet them especially in the Acts of the Apostles and the letters of Paul, certainly seem to have spoken of the outpouring of God's Spirit in these last days primarily in terms of tangible effects; effects perceptible in the natural order, not only in the 'inner life', healings and inspired utterance as well as a renewed sense of God. As we have already seen, the distinctiveness of being a Christian was inseparably bound to distinctive experience, and, to a degree which some modern Christians outside the charismatic movement might find somewhat alien, to 'works of power'. It is not surprising that, as Paul's Corinthian correspondence suggests, the free exercise of spiritual power, in this very concrete sense, had come to be seen in some communities as the central business of the Christian assembly. Gifts are given for use; and the gifts of the Spirit cry out for exercise and expression.

Paul's critique of such an assumption, especially in 1 Corinthians, is centred upon the question of what it is that the gifts are given for. They are for the building up of a community; not just community in general, but a specific sort of community whose identity is defined and characterized by being 'in Christ'. What this means in concrete moral terms is spelled out in 1 Corinthians 13, where love is presented as the context within which all particular spiritual gifts are exercised and by which they are tested. All must employ their gifts for the health of the Church, and that health is precisely a matter of looking to the interests of each other, sensitivity to each other's needs, material and otherwise, giving place in love to each other. There may be a pressure felt to exercise and express what the Spirit is thought to be giving, the pressure to use 'tongues' for praise in the assembly, or to correct the immature Christian practice of another in matters of dietary regulations (1 Cor.8; 10-12;14; Rom.14-15), but this must be subordinated to deeper priorities, common priorities. The shape of the Church's life must be moulded by a bearing with and attending to each other, a reverence for the other as object of Christ's costly love (Rom.14. 1-12,15; 1 Cor.8.11). What the form of Christian life together must make visible is that kind of relatedness, a condition in which rights and individual assertion are ruled out. There is no need for assertion because God has already and authoritatively affirmed the worth of human being through the divine action in Christ, which is itself an action of renunciation, giving place in love (Rom.15.1ff.; 1 Cor.10.32ff.).

So it would be possible to answer the question 'What is it that is distinctive about the Christian assembly?' in more than one way. At the surface level, there are striking and exciting phenomena to which appeal can be made; but Paul presses the question of their purpose and of the ultimate unifying form of Christian life together. God has poured out the Spirit; but that Spirit is to be understood as an agency making for a unified pattern of life, unified by the way believers reflect God's gift in Christ in their self-gift to one another. The focus of unity is thus God's primary gift of Christ; what shapes and characterizes the unity of Christians is the form, the 'likeness' of Jesus Christ, whose 'mind' the community shares (1 Cor.2.16; Phil.2.5). Thus if it is Spirit that makes the Church what it is, Spirit is what forms the corporate and individual likeness of Christ in us; and we shall not be able to use the language of Spirit without at some stage beginning to speak of Christ. For Paul, *pneuma* can no longer be a word that simply describes an agency from which flow signs and wonders; it is what sets us free to take on the likeness of Jesus. And this is shown in our being able to take on our lips the language of Jesus, calling God *Abba* (Gal.4.6; Rom.8.15), in the sure hope of a comprehensive transfiguration of the whole of our created condition, the whole of our relatedness to each other and the rest of the created material world.

This deepening of insight is not merely an individual quirk of Paul's theology. We may set beside it the way in which the tradition about Jesus itself deals with the question of miracle and power. In Mark especially, miracles are not generally performed in response to requests for manifestation and proof (8.11f., 11.27ff.); they are specific acts of compassion (1.41) or, occasionally, prophetic or warning signs (11.12ff., 20ff.). They are bound up with the whole work of showing and proclaiming the kingdom, and so with the general demand for repentance and faith. In Matthew, the healing miracles are signs of the presence of a time of crisis and fulfilment (11.2ff.), the incipient presence of the rule of God (12.28). They are a challenge and a promise, but not a simple guarantee of authority any more than they are in Mark. They are there in virtue of the kingdom, for its sake, and the essential point about the kingdom is the restoration of a people gathered, accepted and healed by God.

The gospel narratives, of course, are written by people who believe that in their life together the rule of God is being exercised through the Lordship of the risen and exalted Jesus: they believe themselves to be living in the more immediate presence of God's rule that is the result of Jesus' resurrection. The promise and preaching of Jesus in his ministry is set in the light of that sequence of events which creates the Church, the events of Easter. The Lord of the Church, in loyalty to whom we live under the victorious rule of God, so that we are delivered from the rule of sin and the death-dealing powers of this present age, is a Lord who has entered upon his kingdom through agony and death. Thus the signs that point to the kingdom in Jesus' ministry are to be interpreted ultimately out of the experience of a divine rule that is achieved through surrender, loss, powerlessness. The miracles are indeed works of power; but to understand that power in its fullness we must understand, on the one hand, how it works at its critical moment, by absorbing hatred and rejection without defence

or retaliation, and what it works towards, a community of reconciliation.

The new world of the Christian community, then, in
which God rules and God's Spirit is shed abroad, is a world
whose forms and meanings depend on the reality of a power
that 'loses' itself to bring about its purpose; and that purpose
is a community of persons built up, nurtured and bound together by the same reality of self-gift in its daily transactions.
What unites and shapes this community is thus continuous
with what it is that shapes and defines the work of Jesus in its
completeness, its paschal fulfilment. To raise, with Paul, the
question of the final purpose of activity that is seen as Spirit-
directed is to open up the whole issue of how God's purpose is
made actual and effective in the history of flesh and blood.
Once we have asked about the context of the more dramatic
experiences of the Spirit that seem to have been so formative
for many early communities, we are on the way to asking
questions about Christology. How are we to speak of the
Spirit in relation to Jesus, in whom God's purpose is
supremely and creatively embodied in our flesh and blood?

The Spirit of the community is the Spirit of Jesus; so much
is regularly taken for granted. At the level of works and manifestations, this can mean no more than that believers have
access to the same sources of power as Jesus; their signs and
healings validate their claim to be of 'one spirit' with the
Lord. But if we now take seriously what has been said about
the inadequacy or ambiguity of wonders in themselves, and
about the context of the kingdom in which alone these
wonders make sense, then the unity of 'Spirit' between Jesus
and the community must involve more than simply the production of comparable miracles. Close to the heart of Paul's
conception of the Spirit (indeed of his whole understanding of
the life of faith) is the idea of the formation in believers of the
likeness of Christ – as we have seen in the first section of this
chapter. Most specifically, believers are drawn into the same
relation with God as is exemplified in Jesus. Jesus called God
Abba, and his whole identity for God and before God rests

upon this assumption that the God of Israel can be confidently addressed as a loving parent. The gospels underline this in many different ways, from the repeated 'My heavenly Father' of Matthew to the profound statements of identity in will and action between Jesus and the God of Israel in the fourth gospel. The tradition shared by Matthew and Luke preserves the prayer taught by Jesus to his disciples, the 'Our Father', which carries in it the assumption that Jesus' relation with God is something we are enabled to take on; and this receives its most far-reaching expression in the Farewell Discourses of John 13-17.

So Paul can give a very exact meaning to the notion that God gives us the 'Spirit' of Jesus who is the Son of God; and in Galatians 4 a further crucial link is made. We have the Spirit of God's Son and are authorised to call God *Abba* as did Jesus; this represents the gift to us of an inheritance of liberty and authority. To be in the relation that entitles us to call God *Abba* is to be delivered from slavery, in particular, from an anxious servitude to the forms and conventions of cultic practice. These (Paul believes) belong to a dispensation which is only provisional and which derives from spiritual powers of lesser authority, not from the true God alone, the God whose own freedom is the source of covenant and promise. Perhaps even more powerful is the cluster of images in 2 Corinthians 3. The life God promises in covenant is given by the Spirit in a relation in which all 'veils' are removed between us and God; in this directness of relationship is to be found liberty, and that liberty is the reflection of God's glory in the life of the believer.

But what is that liberty, that glory, as it appears in the life of Jesus himself? For the fourth gospel, it is the liberty to do the Father's will in laying down his life; the Son of Man is glorified in his betrayal and death. Even in Mark, it is striking that it is in Gethsemane that we find Jesus addressing God as *Abba* as if it is this and the events which follow that show the heart of his relation to his Father. In this light, the work of God's Spirit relates closely to Paul's insight about power made perfect in weakness. The humanity that is shaped by God's Spirit is defined in connection with the cross. The new humanity is, as we have seen, dependent on a power that achieves its ends by sacrifice. More specifically, we can now say that the union of believers with Jesus is also a union in vulnerability: God attains what God purposes in Jesus and in us through the full confrontation of the violence of the human world and the mortality of the human condition itself. And the paradox of belief is that freedom and authority, the 'empowering' of the Christian life, rest upon a primary act of surrender to death. Jesus is raised to share the Father's freedom and authority through holding back nothing in his obedience. To be with him in glory is to share 'a death like his' (Rom.6.5; 2 Cor.4.10f.).

To be 'like God' then, to share and manifest God's glory is to be set free from the fantasy that we can and must attain invulnerability and mastery, that we can fashion a context for ourselves without 'ragged edges' and risks. As the story of Adam and Eve hints, the human temptation to be godlike rests on the longing for an immortality that will set us free from all the constraints of the body, the world, death, other people; but God's gift of Godlikeness gives freedom within these things – the freedom of Jesus. This is a freedom for relationship, community, the freedom proper to the kingdom of God, the people of God. If 'Spirit' is what makes the Christian people distinctive, Spirit is what creates a personality free for love, mutuality, creativity, free within the bounds of life in the world, not promising some conquest or escape from it.

This is expressed in the link made between the Spirit and Christian initiation (1 Cor.12.13; Eph.4.4f.). The descent of God's Spirit is a clear and central motif in the traditions about Jesus' own baptism, and the Lukan accounts of Christian baptism confirm that it was natural to look for manifestations of the Spirit's work in connection with initiation. However, Jesus' baptism is an 'initiation' into the whole of the mission that culminates in the cross; and Paul insists that if baptism is an identification with Jesus, it is an entry into the process of

cross and resurrection. Baptism and the other features of initiation represent the beginning of that life in which Christ is
formed; if the Spirit of God forms Christ in us, the Spirit is
what is at work in our symbolic sharing in Jesus' cross and
resurrection at our initiation. Here we begin to live in the
Spirit, not primarily because extraordinary gifts instantly
manifest themselves, but because the liberation of our humanity for life among God's people, the liberation accomplished in
Jesus' death and resurrection, becomes real for us and in us.

The liberation effected by Easter is pure gift to humanity;
but since cross and resurrection are inseparable from the whole
of Jesus' ministry, we are led to say that the whole of Jesus'
life is likewise pure gift. He is not an exemplary wonder-
worker, but neither is he simply an example of liberated or
Spirit-filled humanity. We receive our liberation as a result of
his gift of himself to his Father in his life and death. It is thus
Jesus who creates the conditions for our re-creation. And if so,
his life is not just a pattern for us to imitate: our ability to
grow into his likeness depends on his initiative, not ours, his
gift, not just our innate capacities. Our relation to him is
always going to be asymmetrical. We receive the Spirit as a
transforming power in our lives because of the work done for
us in the living and dying and rising of Jesus.

If the whole of Jesus' identity is God's gift to us in this
way, Jesus' relation to the Spirit cannot be exactly like ours.
He is the source from which the Spirit's power flows to us; he
is the definition of what life in the Spirit is like, and he is also
the means whereby that life becomes liveable in the world, in
us. We have to say that in one sense Jesus lives out our human
vocation to be children of God, as some theologians have put
it; but that in another sense he lives 'naturally' what we have
to learn. To be a human child of God, without interruption,
without unfaithfulness, to receive and express the purpose of
God in the midst of human pain and vulnerability without
turning aside, without our ordinary experience of grace as a
gradual overcoming of our native fear and destructiveness –
this is what is seen in Jesus. This is why the gospels, although

they present the story of the baptism of Jesus as a crucial moment of decision and a point of entry into deeper awareness of the Spirit's work, do not suggest that the baptism is a moment of conversion, of entry into a new life at odds with what has gone before. They show this event rather as the uncovering of what has always been there in Jesus, since his birth or conception. Even Mark, who has no stories of Jesus' birth, treats the baptism as the event which simply inaugurates Jesus' preaching; we have already been told who he is, in the first verse of the gospel; and there is no hint of a dramatic summons and change, lifting Jesus out of the life he previously leads. He *is* the Son of God, and John's baptism merely anoints the Son for bringing his mission to fulfilment.

Jesus is already what we are called to be: already and forever ahead of us. Our human vocation now comes to us through him. We could sum this up by saying that in him God's calling to the world and the world's response to God are fused together: there is no gap between the first and the second. The human yearning of Jesus to give himself to the Father and see God's will done (e.g. Lk.12.50) is completely at one with God's own yearning to bring the world back home (to God). In Jesus, God is at work in the longing for God. It is this idea that has led Christians from the earliest days of their faith to say that Jesus of Nazareth cannot be spoken of only in terms of a human identity; he embodies or represents something about God. This is the origin of the doctrine of the incarnation, the Christian belief that in Jesus the source of his acts and indeed of his very being from moment to moment is the eternal Son or Word of God. If God acts decisively in the life of Jesus, God is a God who acts not only in giving but also in responding: God acts to heal us and to call us and to re-create us through an act of responding, through the loving self-surrender of Jesus to his Father's purpose; if we take this seriously, we must conclude that God's life is not just an act of pure giving but also somehow includes the receiving and giving back of love. Jesus is able to live out the life he does, not because he has 'invented' the kind of human life that best pleases God by his own imagination, but because his humanly free obedience and love are borne along, shaped and sustained, from the first moment of his existence, by the eternal reality of God's loving response to God's own love, God's delight in God. Jesus is the reality of God's love for God passed through the prism, we might say, of a suffering and struggling human reality.

So Jesus *is* a 'Spirit-filled' human being, one in whom God's Spirit has achieved a masterwork, a wholly consistent life of loving freedom towards God; but he is thus because what is being formed and shaped in Jesus' human life is the likeness of an already-existing perfection, God's loving answer to God's own generosity. The Spirit shapes in Jesus the life of the everlasting Word. It is this life, of course, which the Spirit seeks to shape in all of us; but before we are free to grasp it, to hear God's summons to be daughters and sons of a divine parent, we must be set free and have our eyes opened by a life that shows both the divine call and the possibility of living out a full response to it, and which takes away, by the great absolution pronounced in cross and resurrection, the fear and slavery of sin which keeps us from our true vocation. As the incarnate Word, Jesus both receives the Spirit, energizing the life of the eternal Word in this specific human body and soul, and gives the Spirit, pouring out the gift he has been given. He gives freely because he has received wholly; he has authority to give because he is himself caught up in God's own generosity. The Spirit is both the gift and promise of the Father and the gift of the risen Jesus (e.g. Lk. 24.49; John 14.16,26; 15.26). If Jesus is the supremely 'Spirit-filled' person, this does not mean that he has unrivalled capacities for miracle and mastery, or even that he is a supreme example of selfless love, but that he is the one around whom the community of God's sons and daughters is gathered, gathered by the creative power he bestows, the life of the Holy Spirit.

In recent years, some distinguished theologians, above all Geoffrey Lampe, have proposed that we should qualify our commitment to a trinitarian theology and think instead of a theology of 'God as Spirit' (as in the title of Lampe's Bampton lectures and subsequent book). 'Spirit' is simply a term for God's outreach to the world, and Jesus is the highest embodiment of that outreach. There is much insight in this; it is certainly true to say that the Bible encourages us to think of the Spirit as that which makes God's life active and accessible outside the being of God in itself. But it should be clear how what we are outlining here differs from such a view. We have insisted that when the divine life is thus given in and by the Spirit, what is given is a life that is already in movement and relationship. God is the giving life of the one Jesus calls Father; and God is also the responding life that is shown in Jesus as Son. In relation to the world, God gives the divine life by giving access to the divine response, the divine joy, that is defined in Jesus, the Word made flesh.

But there remains a problem about the Spirit's own status. It may seem as if we now have a Godhead of two identifiable terms, 'Father' and 'Son', plus a rather nebulous power flowing from them. Is this really a trinity? A lot of theological language, especially in the western tradition, has given this impression, and Eastern Orthodox theologians have often pointed out the danger of reducing the Spirit to an impersonal thing, rather than a substantive, purposive agency. It is easy to see why a writer like Augustine could describe the Spirit as *donum,* the gift which the Father and the Son give each other, and give to the world: this is imagery deeply rooted in the biblical ideas we have been exploring in this chapter. But in isolation it can indeed be misleading; and it may well be that the comparative neglect of the theology of the Spirit in a lot of western European theology until fairly recently has something to do with the notion that the Spirit is not the same sort of entity as the Father and the Son. But on what grounds, then, do we talk of the Spirit as a Person in the Trinity?

We must take care not to be misled by the word Person. 'Father' and 'Son' are words which easily lend themselves to images of personality rather like our own personal being, while 'Spirit' does not. But once we realise that we are speaking of realities that eternally constitute each other in their relationships to each other, we should be able to see that 'Father' and 'Son' are more than just magnified human-type consciousnesses; and this may help us to see also that 'Spirit' is not necessarily any less 'personal' in the sense appropriate to God than the other two terms. Certainly it is not adequate to say that the Spirit is just a function of two more vividly or concretely presented subjects. But how exactly are we to think of this distinct eternal reality we call the Holy Spirit? We can describe the Spirit's work in the process of redemption – in the life, death and resurrection of Jesus, and in the experience of believers who are being re-created in the likeness of Jesus. This is what traditional theology termed the 'mission' of the Spirit. But characterizing the eternal life of the Spirit in relation to Father and Son – the 'procession' of the Spirit in the Trinity – is far harder. We cannot, in the nature of the case, expect to arrive at a neat and final solution: trinitarian theology is not like that. But there are two sets of ideas and images that may give us some clue.

First of all, affirming the independent reality of the Spirit tells us that the perfect mutual love of Father and Son, the completeness of giving and receiving in God, is not all that should be said about the divine life. There is no hint of an exclusive mutual absorption: the life of God is also an eternal movement of self-sharing, so that the relation of Father and Son is open to a world of possible beings. God is the primary gift of the Father's love; God is the perfect responding to and mirroring of that love as Word or Son; and God is the gift, to all that lies beyond the divine life, of a share in that fullness of response. It is not that God is compelled to create, but that there is in the richness and perfection of divine life a natural and irreducible momentum towards the sharing of that life, a divine longing for the life of God to be lived in the world that God's love creates in freedom.

But this may still sound as though the Spirit is somehow

subordinate, an 'extra' to the primary reality of Father and Son; so these notions must be balanced or supplemented by a second set of ideas. We encounter God the Spirit in the 'overflow' towards us of the life of Father and Son; but the relation of Father and Son already shows the divine momentum towards sharing, in the Father's pouring out of the divine life to the Son. Should we then think of the Spirit as the ground of this self-sharing by the Father? One modern Orthodox theologian (Paul Evdokimov) has said that the idea of the Spirit proceeding from the Father and the Son would be acceptable only if we could also say that the Son comes forth from the Father *and the Spirit.* This is to say that the Father's act of bringing the Son to birth is not an arbitrary movement arising out of some abyss of divine will, but is in accord with the eternal fact of the divine impulse to self-sharing, something which is not simply identical with either Father or Son, but a distinctive note or moment in the harmony of divine action. In this perspective, the Spirit is what makes the Father-Son relationship itself possible, as well as what makes this relation open to a world in which images of God's life are established.

None of this 'explains' the life of God as Trinity. It serves to open our eyes to the fact that we cannot do trinitarian theology without reflecting on the Holy Spirit as that which *completes* the coherence of the divine life – that in virtue of which God is an everlasting movement of *giving away.* The Father gives life to the Son, the Father and the Son give their life to the world, the creation gives itself in praise to the Father through the Son; and what makes this one single act of God's love is the unity of the Holy Spirit, working in both divine and created love.

The debate that divided eastern from western Christendom as to whether the Spirit proceeds from the Father (as in the original Nicene Creed) or from the Father and the Son (*filioque,* as in the later Latin versions) has some bearing here. Eastern Christians still hold that the *filioque* is symptomatic of the weaknesses of western theology, obscuring the distinctiveness of the Spirit, and making the Spirit inferior, absorbing it into the Father and the Son. As we have noted, there is some substance to this charge. But some modern defenders of the *filioque* have insisted that we must not divorce our language about the Spirit from the Father's purpose to bring creatures into the life of the Godhead by adopting them as sons and daughters in the Son. If we talk about the Spirit in abstraction from this, we are in danger of turning the Spirit into a vague principle of general religiosity. The Spirit's work is to form a Christlike humanity, not simply to spread abroad sensations of the transcendent; to create the relationships that constitute the kingdom of God, not to nurture individual religious intensity. The *filioque* may not be the best means of keeping all this in view, and no eastern theologian would quarrel with these insights; but, for all its inadequacy, the controversial formula may have helped some theologians not to lose sight of the proper connection between the Spirit, the kingdom and the work of Christ.

The trinitarian picture has as much to say about us as about God. In defining our vocation in terms of Christ and the eternal Word made flesh in him, we are told that Godlikeness is never a matter of pure independent initiative. There is in God not only perfect giving but perfect responding. Listening, receiving and depending are not contradictions of divine freedom and creativity. Thus we are not obliged to struggle for a life without dependence and receiving if we wish to be free: if God is Trinity, and if the life of Jesus embodies the life of God as response, we shall find our proper creativity and liberty not by distancing ourselves from others but by learning to receive from as well as give to others in a community of mutual interdependence. And if God is Spirit, we are reminded that our very response to God is a channel for God's giving through us to the world: our growth in the likeness of Christ is inseparable from the mission of the Holy Spirit, in whom the life of God and God's children is constantly widening out to the horizon of the whole creation. To speak in a certain way of God's nature on the grounds of God's action in revelation is to commit ourselves to a particular vision of our calling in the world; this is why the theology of the Trinity is far from being a matter of detached speculation.

What has been outlined in the preceding section clearly bears on our thinking about the Spirit in creation. A certain amount has been written about the Spirit as the agent of God's presence in the created order at large (outside the bounds of the visible Church), building on the fact that, in the Old Testament and Apocrypha, 'Word', 'Wisdom' and 'Spirit' are sometimes overlapping expressions for God's presence and agency in the orderliness and beauty of creation (e.g. Wis. 9,1f., 9,17; and perhaps Gen. 1.2 and Ps.33.6), and 'Spirit' may be connected with the skill of the craftsman in making objects of beauty (Ex.35.31). On this basis, it seems possible to develop a theology of the Spirit at work in art and science, the formation of beauty and the discovery of order, as we attempt in Chapters 8 and 9 of this study. However, for this to avoid the pitfall of once again making the Spirit only a general force for self-transcendence, it needs to be related to what we have described as the primary focus of the insights of the New Testament about the Spirit.

Spirit is the agency that communicates to creatures the possibility of calling God 'Abba', as Jesus called the God of Israel, so that we may speak of the Spirit as the 'overflowing', the outpouring into that which is not God of the divine relationship of gift and response shown to us in Jesus' relation with his Father in heaven. (For this theme of 'outpouring' in visual form, see especially Plate 6). Spirit of God acting to draw creation towards the fullness of the trinitarian life. Thus the Spirit's presence and work should not be seen only in the transfiguration of human lives. Creation as a whole responds to God by being itself; it gives glory to God by reflecting back to God something of the divine beauty, abundance and rationality. If the orderliness, the intelligibility, of the world is its share in the reality of God as Logos, then the variety and resourcefulness of the concrete actuality, the life, of creatures has to do with the reality of God as Spirit. The life of the natural world is disfigured in all kinds of ways, and often

appears to us as terrible, hostile or meaningless. But part of
the good news Christians proclaim is that at the heart of
things, God remains faithfully at work, drawing all things
Godward; and we are never wholly robbed of the capacity to
see creation as a single movement towards God, an act of cosmic 'praise'. The implications of this will be explored further
in our chapter 'The Spirit and Creation'. For the present we
shall note only that such a model of creation-as-praise may
help us to see how the Word that is incarnate in Jesus can be
called the 'beginning' or 'first principle' of all creation. The
Word of God in eternity, Jesus of Nazareth in time, show
what it is for God's will to share the divine life, to have 'free
play', for that will wholly to realise itself. The whole of creation moves towards this realization which is already accomplished in the incarnate Word, the perfect act of praise or
glorification. Paul in Romans 8.22ff. speaks of the 'labour
pains' of creation waiting for the realization of God's freedom
within the world of space and time; and that waiting and
longing is the urging of the Spirit. For the believer, the
mystery hidden from all ages, God's purpose to bring into
eternal life many sons and daughters, reconciled to God, to
each other, and to the whole of their environment, has now
been revealed, and those whose eyes have been opened to it
'were sealed with the promised Holy Spirit' (Eph.1.13). By
the 'pledge' of the Spirit (2 Cor.5.5; Eph.1.14) the created life
of the present age becomes the life of God's future: it enacts
and shows the goal purposed by God for all creation, because
it reflects the life lived out in Jesus. The Old Testament promise to which reference is made in Acts 2.17, that God will
pour out the Spirit in the last days, is fulfilled in the creation
of that Christlike life that is both free of the slaveries and sins
of the present age, and yet wholly committed to finding and
serving God in the present moment.

We have said that there is a Christological criterion by
which the 'achievements' of the human spirit' must be tested.
The same is even more clearly true where Christian spirituality
and Christian sanctity are concerned. We have some fairly

clear standards of discernment for the 'spiritual life' if we consider how human identity is moulded by God's Spirit in that life where it has free play. To the extent that some traditional ideals of humility have produced immaturity and dependence in Christian lives, we must question whether they are truly related to the life of the Spirit. They can produce people for whom dependence means an obsessive conviction of inferiority, people who lack the capacity to take responsibility as adults for their actions. A particular sort of convent spirituality has been specially prone to this; and in the works and life of a great monastic reformer like Teresa of Avila, we can see the tension between the culturally imposed ideals of humility for women religious and the bold conviction that proper dependence on God makes one a friend, not a slave, and equips one for courageous resistance to various kinds of cultural tyranny.

But equally, the ideal of the 'moral athlete', the person struggling towards self-mastery, afraid of exposing vulnerability and admitting need, stands under the judgement of the Spirit's work in Jesus Christ. Jesus does not avoid the pain of admitting human need, as when he begs the disciples to watch with him in Gethsemane; in relation to those whom he comes to redeem, 'he is not ashamed to call them brethren' (Heb.2.11). His is not a humanity seeking perfection in isolation and independence. There is nothing here of what Eliot called 'the fear of belonging'. Those who cannot 'belong' to and with others and God may show it in various ways, for instance the dread of making human commitments, the unwillingness to share problems, even the obstinate insistence that there are no problems in one's relation to God and others that cannot be solved by will. Catholic ideals of priestly spirituality have often fostered just such a suspicion of sharing, just such isolation, fear of admitting need, and concentration on will; and this has played an important part in setting the priest at an emotional as well as a social and cultic distance from the laity. But there is also a Protestant tradition of being reluctant to admit the role of the body and its senses in worship, and nervous about raw emotion. The charismatic movement has been the vehicle of a true judgement of the Holy Spirit upon moralistic and cerebral styles of evangelical piety.

But the critique does not stop here. 'Charismatic' devotion in turn raises the problem how the believer integrates the experiences of loss or absence as well as those of nurture, support and guidance into a whole pattern of discipleship. A relentless insistence that what is normative for Christian experience is what is clear, unambiguous and positive can push the pendulum back towards another kind of dependency or infantilism. Here, in fact, we return to the starting point of this chapter. The identification of the Holy Spirit's presence with the presence of manifest works of power and total subjective clarity about the will of God must sooner or later come to terms with the tensions about this in the tradition about Jesus, above all the Gethsemane narratives. Any account of how the Spirit is to be discerned in human lives must take in the possibility (to say the least) that the Spirit works also in those circumstances where we are forced to 'take our own authority', to decide and act without a single and simple validation either from subjective certainty, a sense of guidance, or from confirmatory wonders. And it must likewise confront the possibility that this represents not a spiritual deficiency but a moment of costly breakthrough to some fuller maturity. Our reflection on the Spirit's presence and work can be informed by the spiritual tradition most often associated with St John of the Cross, which claims that greater intimacy, fuller union, with God may involve a deep and disorienting loss of the sense of God tangibly and specifically at work, or of God as a discernible 'other'. This is not a denial of the abiding centrality of the concept and experience of relation with God, not a capitulation to the mysticism of absorption or identification; it is simply a recognition that the experiential content of this relation will vary, and that being entrusted by God to decide and act without tangible assurance marks an advance in the intimacy between creator and creature, and so can be interpreted as the Spirit's work in us. It is the moment where suffering

prediction, especially on radical Franciscans and also on society as a whole, even beyond the Middle Ages. The point may be put more generally: the visionary ideals of the Middle Ages as reflected in the new religious orders, or the seriousness of purpose which characterised the Reformation, cannot but offer a severe reprimand to the Church of our own day which, though less corrupt and of gentler spirit, even within the charismatic movement itself seldom displays the sheer verve and enthusiasm of such a past.

However, one difficulty in such appeals to the past is the feeling that the Spirit must be associated with progress, leading us into all truth; consequently it is felt that appeal to the past must necessarily be a retrograde step. Ironically this is an assumption which plagues even those who are prepared to appeal to the past. A recent instance would be the way in which those in favour of the ordination of women frequently refer to the move as a work of the Spirit, while seldom, if ever, do those against this development describe their action in similar terms. Presumably the difficulty lies in the use of the dynamic images of the Spirit to advocate apparently staying where you are. Irrespective of the rights or wrongs of that particular issue, the conservative needs to take seriously the fact that the re-appropriation of the past is never exactly the same on any two occasions. The particular concerns which we bring to some past document or event make us read it in new ways; thus the appeal to the past can be just as new and fresh in its insights for our own generation as appeal to current ideas or to practices elsewhere in the contemporary Church. Also we need to bear in mind that, just as the individual's path towards holiness is not uniform but may regress, so too may that of the Church. This may seem too obvious to need mention, but it is not so often noted that the past can provide the basis of a critique of the Church's present. The sixteenth century Reformation itself was not simply an attempt to return to the purity of the New Testament. Augustine in particular, who lived long after the main lines of the New Testament canon were established, was used as the basis for a critique of contemporary sixteenth century theology. Likewise one of the major factors in the changes of the forms of worship which have taken place in the past twenty years is an awareness of the extent to which the worship of the first millennium differed from that of the second.

Such comments as these make all the more acute an issue hitherto not explicitly raised in this chapter, namely the question of truth. How can we believe that the Spirit will guide the Church into all truth when its history has been so complicated and at times shameful? Our chapter specifically on 'The Spirit of Truth' will draw attention to the numerous ways in which the term might be meant, and the implications of its different uses. Certainly we must be aware of the way in which our own society is dominated by an empirical conception of knowledge; our fellow Christians are thus under pressure to attempt empirical 'proof' through experience of God's activity in our midst. This is not to deny the validity of such experience, only to reassure those who cannot believe it or are unable to find it in their own lives. We have to be careful not to decry the sort of confirmation which comes from the conviction that their own understanding of faith makes coherent and meaningful sense of their lives.

This is of course to concede something to subjectivism, but only in the sense that not every one has the time or the opportunity to examine in depth the complex questions of the foundations of our knowledge. (Nor is it the task of this Doctrine Commission to look at that issue!) Instead this chapter must end with the conviction that if the Spirit's activity in the Church is to be understood in terms of guidance, then this guidance must be leading the Church into what is more than merely subjective truth. Again and again individual members of the Body are being addressed, and although this provides no guarantee that the majority will listen, the patience and persistence of God in the address surely makes it likely that they will. At times the initial impetus seems to come more from outside the Church than within, as we see in the recent examples of the status of women and environmental issues. All this shows the freedom of the Spirit to blow where it wills, a dynamic freedom that blows pre-eminently within the Church and whose very dynamism in both individual and community we ignore at our peril.

6

The Spirit and Power

In the preceding chapter we concentrated on the inner life of the Church and on the work of the Spirit in relation to the sacraments; in the course of that chapter some use was made of dynamic images in our discussion of the Spirit's influence. As this new chapter's title suggests, we shall now take up these dynamic images, develop some of the ideas relating to them and consider some of the problems to which the association of power with the Spirit gives rise. These problems affect variously our own individual lives as Christians, the Church as an institution, and the structures of the secular world. The normal evocations of power (and perhaps some of the instinctive expectations with regard to it) as control, dominance, conquest, manipulation and dismissal of weakness will be challenged. We shall be taken once again to the nerve-centre of Christian faith, namely to the death and passion of Christ, for the cross is the paradigm of the way in which Jesus exercises power. Power does not necessarily consist in ability to effect control. There is a power of love which transforms and liberates; it was this power which, to the eye of faith, was evident, active and triumphant on the cross.

GOD'S POWER, JESUS AND THE SPIRIT

In the scriptures there are many references to God's power, both in creation and towards the people of Israel. In the story of the exodus we read a most outstanding sign of God's power in delivering Israel from Egypt. The whole narrative is studded with accounts of miraculous power: miracles before Pharaoh, the crossing of the Red Sea, the pillar of cloud, the

Illustrations

Plate 4   'The Trinity', by Andrei Rublev, c. 1411.
This famous icon of the 'O.T. Trinity' (cf. Gen.18) expresses with great subtlety and power (through the inclination of the figures and the sense of circular movement between them) the inner communality and mutual reciprocity of the Persons of the Trinity. The Spirit is normally taken to be the figure on the right.

Plate 5   'Trinity in the Eucharist', French MS. 1400-1500.
A representation of the Trinity unusual for the west, where (at this stage) an invocation of the Spirit in the eucharistic prayer was absent. The idea is nonetheless here visually expressed that an encounter with the Trinity in most condensed form comes through the eucharistic elements.

Plate 6   'Christ's monogram in a circle of doves', mosaic from the Baptistery, Albenga, 450-500.
The concentric circles perhaps allude to the triple immersion of baptism, and hence to the Trinity. The overflow of trinitarian life into the baptised is expressed in the doves, symbols both of individual souls and of the Holy Spirit.

ACKNOWLEDGEMENTS

The cover illustration 'Blessed Trinity' by Sr. Marlene Scholz, O.P. is reproduced with her kind permission.

Plate 3. 'The Trinity', a sketch by William Blake, reproduced by permission of the British Library.

Plate 5. 'Trinity in the Eucharist' reproduced by permission of the Bodleian Library, Oxford (MS.Rawl.liturg.e.12.fol.13).

Plate 1.   'Throne of Grace', from the altar of the Wiesenkirche, Soest, c.1250-70.

Plate 2. 'Trinity with "female" Holy Spirit', Urschalling, Bavaria, fourteenth century.

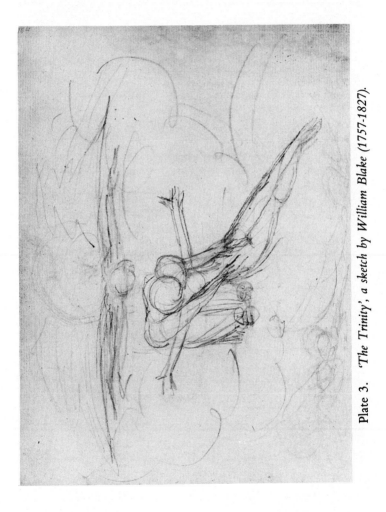

Plate 3. 'The Trinity', a sketch by William Blake (1757-1827).

Plate 4. *'The Trinity', by Andrei Rublev, c.1411.*

Plate 5. *'Trinity in the Eucharist', French MS. 1400-1500.*

Plate 6. 'Christ's monogram in a circle of doves', mosaic from the Baptistery, Albenga, 450-500.

manna in the desert, the water from the rock. In their song to God, Moses and the people of Israel ask, 'Who is like thee, majestic in holiness, terrible in glorious deeds, doing wonders?' (Ex. 15.11).

Yet we must face the fact that some of the instances in the scriptures in which God's power is believed to be at work strike us as arbitrary and cause many people in today's culture to feel ill at ease. For instance, chastisement with blindness is a divine judgement in the Old Testament and the New (2 Kings 6.18; Acts 13.11); striking with leprosy is found in 2 Kings 5.27 and making dumb in Luke 1.20. Further, immunity to poisonous snake bites was provided by divine power when Moses lifted up the brazen serpent in the wilderness and when Paul shook into the fire the snake which had fastened upon him (Num. 21.9; Acts 28.3ff.). The Johannine Jesus refers to this apparent arbitrariness in an enigmatic passage in which he explicitly associates the Spirit with this feature, 'The wind blows where it wills, and you hear the sound of it, but you do not know whence it comes or whither it goes; so it is with every one who is born of the Spirit' (John 3.8).

Some of the passages on which we have just drawn come from the Acts of the Apostles, in which the Spirit is depicted as being powerfully at work in the young Church. In the Acts it is made quite clear that power in the Spirit is always the free gift of God, and never the result either of merit to be rewarded or of consensus choice or of the assuaging of demand. The narrative concerning Simon Magus (Acts 8.9-24) is particularly revealing in this connection. The account distinguishes between the (legitimate) demand that a hunger for God be satisfied, and a desire to take to oneself this particular and unique power. When the power of the Spirit is described as given, in response to the prayer of Peter and John for the believers 'through the laying on of the apostles' hands' (v.18), its effects are such that they go beyond the 'signs and great miracles' (v.13b) which had previously amazed Simon Magus. He had clearly regarded the ability to invoke the gift of the Holy Spirit as a power, and therefore as a commodity, which surpassed any acts or wonders practised or seen by him. His request to purchase this power (v.19) is sharply rejected by Peter, 'Your silver perish with you, because you thought you could obtain the gift of God with money' (v.20). The force of the story is less about sin and more about the nature of the Spirit's power, which is to be invoked only as a gift of God. The emphasis lies on the given nature of the Spirit's empowering; this is not to be won or earned or bought. Turning to the letters of Paul we find precisely the same emphasis. When he was faced with questions about his personal apostolic authority, he insisted that the source of this authority lay in the gift of God; his apostleship was 'not from men nor through man, but through Jesus Christ and God the Father' (Gal.1.1); his call was 'by the will of God' (1 Cor.1.1); and his preaching is 'in demonstration of the Spirit and power' (1 Cor. 2.4b). His power in the Spirit came as divine gift, as did also his converts' life in the Spirit, 'It is God who establishes us with you in Christ, and has commissioned us; he has put his seal upon us and given us his Spirit in our hearts as a guarantee' (2 Cor.1.21f.).

Further, Paul clearly believed his gospel, to be 'in power and in the Holy Spirit' (1 Thess.1.5). We may thus properly speak of the power of the gospel. This phrase expresses both the quality of power which the Spirit gives and also the means by which it is given. At the heart of this power of the gospel lies the experience of being empowered by the Spirit. Jesus himself was empowered by the Spirit at his baptism. The Spirit immediately drove him out into the wilderness (Mark 1.12) and no doubt sustained him in his temptations here. It was 'in the power of the Spirit' that he returned to Galilee (Lk. 4.14). His sermon in the synagogue at Nazareth gives us to understand that his preaching and mighty works were done in the power of the Spirit (Lk. 4.16ff.). Among his mighty works was the casting out of demons; the first three evangelists see the overcoming of occult evil powers as one of the most significant elements in Jesus' ministry and as one which reveals Jesus' unique authority. Already, in Jesus' public ministry we can see two sharply contrasted tendencies: on the one hand there is the exercise of authority, evidence of his being in control, the successful performance of his mission, his work understood in terms of defeat for Satan, who was seen falling from heaven; on the other hand there is also the experience of human weakness, on occasions of failure (e.g. in his home country), in the refusal either to perform cures to order or to coerce acceptance of his message, or in his preference (on occasions) for hidden anonymity. These two contrasted tendencies, of authority and of self-chosen limitation, have to be held together and understood to be contained within the power of Spirit who equipped Jesus for his work and ministry. When we turn to the Lord's passion, the tension between these two contrasted tendencies becomes more acute. On the one hand there is the note, particularly to be found in John's gospel, that the death of Jesus is to be understood in terms of achievement (John 19.30) and triumph (John 16.33), and in all the gospels the tone of authority is to be heard unmistakeably at the Last Supper, at Jesus' arrest and at his trial. On the other hand there is weakness, failure, shame and dereliction, in the passion narratives in all four gospels. The use of glory in John's gospel holds these two emphases together: the glory of God (and that includes the power and self-revelation of God) is to be found at its most powerful and clearest in the shame and failure of the cross. In the light of the resurrection, or through the lens of the resurrection, we see Gethsemane and Calvary to be at one and the same time both the most absolute self-giving, self-emptying beyond human conceiving and also the most absolute vindication, victoriously effecting new life of a kind beyond human conceiving.

Jesus and his passion represent for us the touchstone of the power of which we speak, the means by which it is given, its effects when poured out, and its confrontation with other concepts of power abroad in the world. Christ's action on the cross involved both submission and surrender, two quite distinct categories. He submitted to his Father, and, as a consequence, he surrendered to mortality and humiliation. By contrast, the resurrection involved empowering and being justified. This resurrection power is consequential upon, not accidental to, the act of Christ on the cross. The submission to the will of the Father, which involves for the Son free acceptance of vulnerability to both shame and mortality, is in organic spiritual relationship to the victorious power of the resurrection in the triumphant overcoming of corruptible flesh and in the glorious vindication of the one shamed.

THE SCANDAL OF THE CROSS, AND POWER IN CHRISTIAN LIVES

It has to be said that, in some passages within the New Testament and also not infrequently in subsequent Christian thinking and hymnody, starkly triumphalist language has been used with regard to the earthly ministry of Jesus, to his death and resurrection. In the final chapter of the previous report (*We Believe in God,* pp.147ff.) we tried to do justice both to Christ's weakness and vulnerability and also to his sovereignty and victory, all of which belong to God. It is a veritable scandal, an offence or stumbling block, that both these emphases are so deeply rooted in Christian faith.

At the heart of this Christian faith stands the cross of Christ. Thus we should expect the means by which the Spirit works to be distinguishable from the source and effect of other kinds of power. Particularly in Paul's epistles we find the cross of Christ (1 Cor. 1.23ff.), the vocation of Christians (1 Cor. 1.26ff.), the Christian life itself (1 Cor. 4.8ff. and 2 Cor 12.1ff.) all presented in starkly paradoxical language about power and weakness. He insists that the Spirit's power is to be discovered and demonstrated in the context of human weakness freely accepted and offered to God. Indeed, it would be no exaggeration to say that in the first four chapters of his first letter to the Corinthians Paul is revaluing the nature of power. One of his most daring assertions occurs in this passage: 'I decided to know nothing among you except Jesus Christ and him crucified. And I was with you in weakness and in much fear and trembling; and my speech and my message were not in plausible words of wisdom, but in demonstration of the Spirit and power, that your faith might not rest in the wisdom of men but in the power of God' (1 Cor. 2.2ff.). In these verses he makes explicit the connection between, on the one hand, the power of the Spirit and the Christian's acceptance of human vulnerability and, on the other hand, the power which flows from Christ's own acceptance of human vulnerability and its overcoming in his resurrection. Christ's raising from the dead is of the same order as the transformation of the disciples, through the Spirit, from a defeated rabble into a dynamic and centrally bonded group of witnesses speaking with authority. Acknowledgement of, even willing surrender to, the reality of human weakness is the only condition for our receiving the power of the Spirit, provided that this acknowledgement and this surrender are accompanied by a total commitment of faith to the God and Father of our Lord Jesus Christ.

Already this treatment of power and weakness in the ministry of Jesus, in his death and resurrection and in the earliest Christians' experience of the Spirit has led us to wider consideration about the nature of the Christian life. We have already remarked that in the early chapters of 1 Corinthians Paul is re-evaluating the nature of power; in so doing, he is laying the foundation for his treatment of the corporate life of the Church in chapters 12 to 14. Elsewhere in this study we have referred to particular elements in this treatment (e.g. pp. 48ff.). Here we note that the Church's experience of the Spirit's power goes hand in hand not with the search for ascendancy, but with submission to God, even the acceptance of the reality of the cross as its way of being.

In the middle of the passage from Paul's first letter to the Corinthians, to which we have just referred, we find the anatomy of charity in Chapter 13. Once again we find a markedly Christocentric reference. That chapter with its picture of suffering, gentle, indestructible love reminds irresistibly of the figure of the gospels and must surely have been shaped by

Paul's reflection on the traditions which he had received concerning 'the Son of God, who loved me and gave himself for me' (Gal. 2.20). 'Love is patient and kind; love is not jealous or boastful; it is not arrogant or rude. Love does not insist on its own way; it is not irritable or resentful; it does not rejoice at wrong, but rejoices in the right. Love bears all things, believes all things, hopes all things, endures all things' (1 Cor. 13. 4ff.).

In this picture there is no space for self-aggrandizement, or for self-assertion at the expense of others. The fruit of the Spirit in its various elements, 'love, joy, peace, patience, kindness, goodness, faithfulness, gentleness, self-control' (Gal.5.22f.), exhibits the power which flows from submission to God in Christ and from self-abnegation. This fruit is contrasted with the various works of the flesh (Gal. 5.19ff.; see also Col. 3.5,8) which all are evidence of self-assertion and of a distorted use of power. The Christocentric element remains: life in the Spirit and in the body of Christ is progressively shaped by conformity, through obedience and suffering, to the image and likeness of Jesus Christ. Wherever they are found, the various elements in the fruit of the Spirit are to be attributed to God's creative generosity, for when the Church's members are true to their calling, this fruit is particularly capable of being evoked, nurtured, sustained, made concrete, shaped and given identity by the Spirit of Christ within the body of the Church.

EMPOWERING BY THE SPIRIT

We have already perceived that acknowledged weakness is a continuing condition of the Spirit's empowering. Now we identify some of the means by which this power is communicated. First in importance among the means by which the power of the Spirit is received is the experience of God's forgiveness. Forgiveness and restoration to fellowship with God are conditional on repentance. On the day of Pentecost

Peter preached to the crowd, 'Repent and be baptized every one of you in the name of Jesus Christ for the forgiveness of your sins; and you shall receive the gift of the Holy Spirit' (Acts 2.38). Peter's message was in direct continuity with the preaching of Jesus during his earthly ministry, 'Repent, and believe in the gospel' (Mk. 1.15) and with his ministry of forgiveness and restoration to physical and spiritual wholeness: 'My son, your sins are forgiven... Rise... and walk' (Mk. 2.5,9). This forgiveness is closely linked with the climax of Jesus' ministry, on the cross. Through the crucified and risen Lord God dispenses the Spirit and empowers the disciples to exercise, through this gift of the Holy Spirit, that same ministry of God's forgiveness which they had received from Jesus himself (John 20.19ff.). This forgiveness, which is inseparably associated with Jesus' death, is repeatedly to be made available afresh within the fellowship of the Eucharist (Matt.26.28). Further, Paul in his preaching and teaching insists that God's forgiveness through Christ is something given, the acceptance of which opens the channel of empowering for new life (e.g. Acts 13.39; 26.18; Rom. 4.7; Col. 1.14).

The verse from Peter's speech on the day of Pentecost to which we have just referred links baptism with repentance as one of the primary means by which the reality of forgiveness is reinforced by the gift of the Spirit. In the preceding chapter we discussed the significance of baptism in this regard. For the present we note that baptism marks for Christian believers a radical shift from destructive self-centredness and isolation into a belonging to the Christian fellowship which is no mere coming together of like-minded individuals, but is a condition of the new life itself. 'By one Spirit we were all baptized into one body ... and all were made to drink of one Spirit' (1 Cor. 12.13). The power of the Spirit effects in the believer incorporation into a living body, the living body of Christ. Integration into the saving events of the cross and resurrection and integration into the body of Christ, the living fellowship of the Spirit, are one and the same act.

Within the New Testament we find other means whereby the power of the Spirit is given and received. Important among them is preaching; this is discussed as a means by which the Spirit acts in power. Moreover the power of the Holy Spirit may be invoked in various ways; particular examples are the laying on of hands, the handkerchief of Paul, even the shadow of Peter. Common to all these means, to forgiveness and baptism as well, is a category which is the prior channel of the Spirit's power and which is at the centre of the New Testament's account of power: namely, that of believing. All four gospels mark Jesus' own insistence on believing as the only condition within which his works of power can take place, and even Jesus was restricted in his ministry by lack of faith in his hearers (Mk. 6.5f.). The importance attached by the early Church to believing as a condition of receiving the Spirit and as an authoritative channel of the power of the Spirit can be gauged from the narrative in Acts 10 and 11, which records Peter's extension of baptism to the Gentiles. This extension is accredited by the initially sceptical church at Jerusalem on the grounds that the Spirit had been given through their believing. Peter preaches to the Gentile Cornelius, '"To him (Jesus Christ) all the prophets bear witness that every one who believes in him receives forgiveness of sins through his name." While Peter was still saying this, the Holy Spirit fell on all who heard the word' (Acts 10. 43f.). 'If then', Peter later demanded of the church at Jerusalem, 'God gave the same gift to them as he gave to us when we believed in the Lord Jesus Christ, who was I that I could withstand God?' (Acts 11.17).

Believing is indeed a condition of receiving the Spirit: yet at the same time the New Testament asserts, and we are bound to assert, that believing is itself the gift of God and the effect of the Spirit's work in us. Within believing we include both trust in the object of belief and also faith understood as the capacity to receive and to appropriate God's gifts. In both respects this believing is the gift of God to us; 'No one can say "Jesus is Lord" except by the Holy Spirit' (1 Cor. 12.3); 'By grace you have been saved through faith; and this is not your own doing, it is the gift of God' (Eph. 2.8).

Here we meet one of the major difficulties in speaking about the Spirit and power, that of distinguishing cause from effect. The problem could be stated in terms of the need to distinguish both what the power of the Spirit has effected in the lives of the Christian fellowship, and the means by which that power has been received. Both the New Testament and also the tradition and experience of the Church indicate that believing gives openness to or recovery of the power of the Holy Spirit; yet it is the power of the Holy Spirit which enables people to believe. Further reflection makes us aware that these distinctions are, in a sense, unreal: insofar as the power of God at work in the world through the Spirit is that power which was at work both on the cross and in the Easter garden, cause and effect are one; obverse and reverse of the same unimaginable action.

We have already touched on the ethical consequences of life in the Spirit, both for the individual believer and for the Christian community. In Paul's epistle to the Galatians we find an emphasis on the Spirit both as the gift of God, empowering disciples to realize their sonship, and also as God's summons to a totally Christlike obedience. 'God sent forth his Son ... so that we might receive adoption as sons. And because you are sons, God has sent the Spirit of his Son into our hearts, crying, "Abba! Father!"' (Gal. 4. 4ff.). That gift of the Spirit does not relieve us of the responsibility of living the life of faith which is the consequence of our sonship. Thus the Spirit is also that power by which believers are summoned to regulate their lives. 'If we live by the Spirit, let us also walk by the Spirit' (Gal. 5.25).

If as believers we find our new life in Christ who for us was crucified and raised again, then we also live in the Spirit who reveals that same Christ to us and empowers us with his salvation. The Spirit works within us both in creating our faith and also in requiring substance to our life as Christians. By substance we mean a certain quality of being and behaviour, which is recognizably Christlike. If the kind of power attributable to the Spirit is to be recognizable as power in any sense at all in which the word has common currency, then in some form or other it must have discernible effect. Thus the distinctive quality of 'power' in the Christian life is found in identification with Christ's way of self-emptying, self-sacrifice, suffering in solidarity with all victims of human hurt or natural affliction, and self-oblation to the will of the Father. For out of that will come the self-evidencing authority of righteousness, truth and love. Ultimately, the power that the Spirit gives is the power of love. It was as they beheld his wounds that the risen Christ breathed his Spirit upon his disciples (John 20.20ff.).

All of this may seem a far cry from the actual behaviour of most Christians, in Church history and today. Christians are not always conspicuously remarkable for discernible growth in Christlike qualities. Moreover, the Church as an institution has only too frequently exercised power in ways fundamentally at variance with the insights on which we have been concentrating. This uncomfortable fact does not diminish the strength and urgency of the New Testament's exhortation to us 'to become what we are' in Christ. It does, however, set a humbling paradox, between our potential and what is apparent, at the centre of anything we say about the power of the Spirit in Church. One aspect of this same humbling paradox is the fact that the Church lives both in the present and in a condition of eschatological hope. (We shall return to this theme in our final chapter.) We have the assurance that, both individually and corporately, 'We all ... are being changed into his (Christ's) likeness from one degree of glory to another', and Paul adds, 'This comes from the Lord who is the Spirit' (2 Cor. 3.18).

There is another anomalous element which we note with regard to our new life in the Spirit: from New Testament times the consequences of corporate living by this power of the Spirit have been found both in extraordinary manifestations and the life of the commonplace, the prosaic and the everyday. The pastoral epistles stress the latter (e.g. 2 Tim. 1.7; Tit. 3.1ff.). In his first letter to the Corinthians Paul makes a distinction between gifts such as miracles, healings, tongues and interpretations, on the one hand, and the undramatic, mundane, humdrum gifts such as helping and administering, on the other (1 Cor. 12.28ff.). This point may be seen even more clearly in that other early discussion of spiritual gifts, in Romans 12; here Paul lists prophecy, service, teaching, exhorting, contributing, giving aid, performing acts of mercy (Rom. 12.6ff.). It seems as if Paul is casting his eye around the Christian community and making sure that no one's contribution is overlooked. Moreover, it is 'the same Spirit ... the same Lord ... the same God' (1 Cor. 12.4ff.) who inspires all these gifts in every member of the body. Paul is no doubt attempting to forestall any suggestion that the Spirit may be given in greater measure to some who have certain gifts, and in lesser measure to others with certain other gifts. He emphasizes that the weaker and humbler members, whose gifts may seem nothing to boast about, are all the more essential to the effective working of the body of Christ, just as the 'unpresentable' parts of the human body are modestly concealed, even though they have a particular vital part to play in the healthy function of the whole body (1 Cor. 12.14ff.).

Nevertheless the tradition of 'signs and wonders' following the Spirit in the life of the Christian community is a continuous one, the strength of which is of very great importance not least in the life of today's Church, which has discovered afresh these phenomena of power in the Spirit. We touched on them in Chapter 3 of this study, and it is to a consideration of these phenomena that we now return.

SIGNS AND WONDERS: GOOD AND EVIL POWER

The charismatic movement as a whole has given prominence to what might be called the ecstatic gifts (tongues, interpretation, prophecy) in worship. Certain strains within the move-

ment, however, have emphasized the more dynamic phenomena of healing, exorcism and miraculous words of knowledge in evangelism. Many people find these subjects puzzling
and problematical; in our treatment of them we have borne in
mind a number of general considerations: for instance,
paranormal phenomena of various sorts are found in many
cultures in most periods of history; they are by no means exclusive to the Bible, to the history of the Christian Church, or
to the modern charismatic movement. Moreover, there is no
consensus among Christian people today about the existence
of demons and therefore none about the meaning of possession
and exorcism. This fact is bound to affect any evaluation of
some of the biblical narratives and of some modern claims, but
critical attention and assessment is not to be identified with
faithlessness or with a claim to superior insight. We sit under
scripture in order to discern the word of God, and we attend
to modern claims in order to do proper justice to them.

Against this background we consider the claim to engage in
'power evangelism'. This claim presumably echoes Paul's
boast in the epistle to the Romans that Christ had worked
through him to win obedience from the Gentiles 'by word
and deed, by the power of signs and wonders, by the power of
the Holy Spirit' (Rom. 15.18f.). These phenomena are said to
be very widespread today. Many Christian people join with
religious sceptics in frank disbelief of such claims. For some,
indeed, in a post-Hume era, belief in the miraculous is neither
necessary nor fitting. However, this *a priori* rejection of the
miraculous is by no means the general view in the Church;
therefore, those who do not share it, but rather believe in the
God and Father of our Lord Jesus Christ as the God of
miracle, are called carefully to evaluate claims made in this
area. Running through Christian history is evidence both that
signs and wonders do occur, and also that seeking a sign is not
an imperative of the gospel. In fact many passages in the
gospels actively discourage believers from making such a demand (e.g. Matt. 16.1ff.; John 4.48). We properly enquire
about biblical attitudes to these phenomena and about the way

in which these attitudes bear upon our understanding of the Spirit as power.

As we noted near the beginning of this chapter, God gave a most outstanding sign of power in delivering Israel from Egypt; the exodus itself was, we read, preceded by many remarkable signs and wonders. In the New Testament Jesus is understood as effecting a new exodus. Nearly a third of the gospels is occupied with miracles, from Jesus' miraculous conception to his miraculous resurrection. He was indeed, as Peter affirmed at Pentecost, 'a man attested to you by God with mighty works and wonders and signs which God did through him in your midst' (Acts 2.22). The prophecy of Joel was fulfilled, and at Pentecost the Spirit was poured out on the followers of Jesus.

The sequel, according to the Acts of the Apostles, was a remarkable collection of signs and wonders, given not for show but for furtherance of the gospel. In the New Testament there is both confidence and reticence with regard to signs and wonders, which were perceived to accompany the ministry of Jesus and the early life of the Church. There is no doubt that God gave signs, and there is a sense of wonder at God's self-disclosure. Though references to signs are frequent in the New Testament, only a few of these references present signs and wonders as authenticating evangelism (e.g. Rom. 15.19, to which we have already referred; Heb. 2.4; and, from the longer ending of Mark, Mk. 16.20). Only infrequently are these signs brought before the readers as palpable marks that the Lord is with his disciples. They are indications of his presence and power; the New Testament is clear about that, and so is much contemporary experience, but that is not the principal emphasis in the New Testament.

In this study we have frequently mentioned our Christocentric framework of reference. Precisely this point needs to be made with regard to the miracles done by Jesus. They are mighty acts performed by Jesus primarily in order to show who he is. The fourth gospel is specifically designed to show this; the miracles there are not included to make the reader feel good, nor to amaze the unbelievers, nor even to meet human need. Their function is to glorify God and to bear witness to the Son. In all the signs in John's gospel the act and the interpretation combine to bring the spotlight on Jesus; they indicate who he is and what he can do for humanity. Despite John 14.12 they are not primarily models for his disciples to follow.

Further, signs and wonders do not necessarily come from God. They did not in the case of those worked by Pharaoh's magicians; nor in that of those worked by Jewish wonder-workers who performed exorcisms in the days of Jesus (see Matt.12 24ff.); nor in that of Simon Magus (as we noted earlier), who backed his amazing claims with amazing cures (Acts 8.11). Within the New Testament there are warnings to disciples and believers not to be carried away by signs; we note particularly, 'False Christs and false prophets will arise and show signs and wonders, to lead astray, if possible, the elect. But take heed; I have told you all things beforehand' (Mk. 13. 22f.), and 'The coming of the lawless one by the activity of Satan will be with all power and with pretended signs and wonders' (2 Thess. 2.9). Thus it is not surprising that we are not encouraged to place our faith in signs. The supreme sign presented to us is not God's power in miracle, but God's weakness on a cross.

In any case, signs and wonders do not necessarily produce faith. The account of the early part of Jesus' ministry contained in Matthew's gospel includes many miracles. We read that some of the Scribes and Pharisees asked him, 'Teacher, we wish to see a sign from you' (Matt. 12.38). Jesus condemned their attitude, using language about an evil and adulterous generation. No sign can compel faith, and once again the cross and resurrection of Jesus ('the sign of Jonah') is the supreme sign. Concentration on signs and wonders can cause people to look in the wrong direction and even to value God's gifts more than God.

There is, however, another, deeper reason why signs and wonders by themselves can be misleading. This reason will cause no surprise to the reader who has followed the reasoning of this chapter: Christians must expect the way of the cross as well as the power of the resurrection. During this earthly life Christians are citizens of two countries. We remain 'in Adam', subject to weakness, fallenness, sin, suffering and death. 'In Christ', however, we are open to the power of God's future, that is to justification, deliverance from wrath, the power and gifts of the Holy Spirit; we have even 'tasted … the powers of the age to come' (Heb. 6.5). Thus triumphalism is illegitimate, for we have not yet arrived. Equally defeatism is inappropriate, for we are not where we were; God who has already begun a good work in us 'will bring it to completion at the day of Jesus Christ' (Phil. 1.6). Much mainline Christianity has concentrated exclusively on the power of the resurrection and the present realization of the age to come. Authentic Christianity tries to hold fast to both, taking its cue from Paul who, writing, 'The signs of a true apostle were performed among you in all patience, with signs and wonders and mighty works' (2 Cor. 12.12), had but a few lines earlier written about his thorn in the flesh which he had three times asked the Lord to remove, but in vain.

Our conclusion about signs and wonders, therefore, is that, like so much which we have considered in this chapter, they should be understood as power in weakness. If Jesus Christ suffered on a cross and is our head, there is no way in which the several members of his body will escape hardship and suffering. Equally, there is no way in which the risen Lord will begrudge to his believing followers here in this mortal life some of the powers of the age to come, for the Spirit is the first instalment of heaven.

THE POWER OF THE SPIRIT AND POWER IN THE WORLD

We now consider a rather different set of problems to which the Christian claim to power in the Spirit gives rise. What is the relation between this power in the Spirit and power as generally understood in the world? Power in the world always has an element of ascendancy of material, political or personal force. Authority in the world, to be recognized, must have the substance to make good its claim to direct the community. That substance we call power, and its qualitative nature is that of dominance. When an opposing force rises with greater ability it makes its claims good, then with the passing of dominance it seems that the reality of power as effective in the world also passes, and its authority becomes suspect. We immediately find ourselves faced by the dilemma that the Church, the body of Christ, is also an institution in the world. Yet in the life of the Spirit, power, whether individual or corporate, will be characterized not by dominance but by self-giving. That power which is authoritative and commands acknowledgement shows itself in a way of living. In Christ the way of living appropriate for the Christian community is wholly shaped by individual and corporate self-giving and self-emptying. The community which lives in the Spirit will embody that power in its acceptance of vulnerability and humbleness, serving and lowliness, and in the transformation of these qualities. This fellowship is baptized both with the shame of Christ's death and with the glory of his resurrection. Obedience in the Spirit is both authoritative and self-emptying, glorious as well as lowly.

There is, however, nothing glorious (quite the reverse) about weakness or humiliation in themselves. Sometimes too within the Church there is heard a certain romanticizing of failure and of weakness, even an assumption that the Church should not seek or expect success. In the concluding part of the preceding section of this chapter we touched on this, and here the point needs to be made again, that Christian convictions about the death and resurrection of Christ necessarily make us reconsider the criteria for power and success which most of us instinctively share with the wider world. In the Church we cherish the vision of a will directed, through the Spirit, in Christlike obedience to the Father; such power invests all that it touches, including humiliation, with glory.

Further, Jesus' saying recorded in the fourth gospel, that he has power to lay down his life and power to take it again (John 10.18) reminds us that the power with which we are concerned may, as he did, choose vulnerability in place of dominance. There is an exercise of choice and of the will: we are not talking about resignation or passivity or that feebleness of spirit which makes no choice at all. Equally, we are not looking for a Church in which human qualities such as initiative and drive have no place. Rather, the Christian community, recognizing as authoritative for it the paradoxical character of the power in the Spirit about which we write, may discover this to be the power which binds it against fragmenting, sustains it in the deserts of the world, and moves it forward disturbingly in its freedom.

The Church, however, is human as well as divine, of mortal flesh and of Spirit. The body of Christ as found in this or that group which constitutes a local or national church needs to consider how the real 'power in the Spirit' addresses the real 'power in the world' as it shapes the 'worldly' institution, the Church. It has to face such questions in relation not only to its own institutional existence, but also to the world around it, and so too do its individual members. The Church does in fact face a particular instance of a wider problem: namely, the ambivalence of all power and of all structures wherever they are to be found. No organization can do without structure, organization and authoritative decision-making; formalized patterns of authority are essential for any body, the Church included. Some complain that the structures of the Church cramp the Spirit, others that synods are but the scenes of all too human power struggles, others that the exercise of episcopal authority as a mode of church government is inconsistent with the notes of hiddenness, anonymity and submission to which we earlier referred. All are instances in which power operates: it would do no harm frankly to recognize that power and dominance of this secular, worldly kind are part of that life in the world to which the Church is called, the responsibility for which must not be avoided. Once that is recognized and once it is perceived also that all structures, including ecclesiological ones, are under the Spirit's judgement, then it should be possible to work at imperfect structures and at the way in which power is exercised in our community. There are elements in any institutional structure which may be inimical to the life of the Spirit. Thus much depends on the way in which we operate the structures. There is, in any case, much in the Pauline epistles about the defeat of authorities and powers; they hold no ultimate authority and secure their true end in submission to Christ.

To put it simply: we are summoned by the very nature of our new life in the Spirit neither to avoid the responsibility of power in the world when God lays it on us, nor to seek it. Instead we are called to exercise it in such a way that we accept its burden (for it is heavy), remain unseduced by it, and surrender it when our time for handing it on is complete. Such a response to issues of power for the Church as an institution, and for its individual members both as they live within the Church and as they function in the secular world, raises further questions so large that we can here only sketch three lines of approach to them.

First, both the attitude with which we approach our life in an institutional Church, and also the way in which we answer ingrained patterns of social interaction, can be affected by the power in the Spirit which we have been discussing, and they must be held open to it.

Second, this power in the Spirit will be reflected in the quality of the institutional Church's common life, particularly as it is expressed in the activity of prayer and worship. Here it is that the Church, ever aware of its own weakness and imperfection, is (or should be) particularly open to receiving the power of the Spirit.

Third, the Church, the Church's authority and structures are never ends in themselves, but exist only for the service of God and in dependence on God. Given a firm grasp of this truth, the Church should actually feel itself relieved that it is of little worldly consequence, indeed should delight in and perhaps boast of that fact, that the power of Christ may rest upon it.

Moreover, Christian people who play significant roles in secular institutions and exercise authority and power in the secular sphere may be helped by reflecting on the conviction of the New Testament writers that Christ on the cross deprived secular power and authority of its dominance. This being so, it is for Christian people to remember that any power they hold is, because they are Christian, given to them only to enable them to serve God in the world; that the spirit in which it is exercised counts; and that the quality of life in any institution in which they play a role may be powerfully affected by that Spirit of power in which they have a share and of which we write. These reflections about power and the Spirit lead to our consideration of truth and the Spirit, the subject to which we devote our next chapter.

7
The Spirit of Truth

TRUTH AND THE HOLY SPIRIT

What do we look for when we ask for 'truth'? In the abstract, apart from some given context of enquiry, we can speak more readily of what truth is *not*. It is not falsehood, self-deception, illusion, or unsubstantiated opinion. At first glance, this bears some relationship to Christian understandings of the work of the Holy Spirit. The Holy Spirit exposes falsehoods, dissolves the self-deception of illusions, and witnesses to the truth of God. When he writes, 'it is the Spirit himself bearing witness with our spirit that we are children of God' (Rom. 8.16), among other things Paul is implying that Christians' confidence that they are sons of God is valid, and does not derive from some illusory belief which grew solely from inside their heads.

On further reflection, however, the subject becomes more complex. In the first place, how do we distinguish the witness of the Holy Spirit from merely subjective feelings of conviction or certainty? The witness of the Spirit does not seem to offer some second, independently checkable channel of knowledge which we can identify in distinction from the conviction or belief itself. Indeed the biblical traditions acknowledge without hesitation that claims to be inspired by the Holy Spirit must be examined and critically tested (1 Thess.5.20ff.; 1 John 4.6).

In the second place, what counts as truth may be, or seem to be, a different kind of thing depending on our context of discourse. Is the truth of a poem the same kind of thing as the truth of a newspaper report? This issue is notoriously complex when we face questions about truths of religion in relation to

112

truths of the natural sciences. On one side, we wish to affirm
the unity of the world, the unity of God, and the unity of
truth. An entirely pluralist view of truth which divides reality
into a series of self-contained areas seeks to solve one set of
problems only by ignoring another. Yet we should not expect
that truth about the nature of God or even moral truth about
the self, would be of the same order, or assessed by the same
criteria, as truth about the location or speed of molecules.
Does the activity of the Holy Spirit relate to all, to most, to
some, or to none of these areas?

In the third place, questions about truth call our attention
to what has traditionally been thought of as the problem of
subject and object. Truth has been defined by one writer, Bernard Lonergan as 'a relation of knowing to being' (*Insight,* p.
552). What capacities to judge or to discern does the person
who is seeking to know actually possess? At this point traditional Christian language speaks of the Holy Spirit as being
operative in removing human blindness and preparing a state
of readiness to perceive. But, once again, does this concern all
kinds of truth, or does it relate only to truth in the context of
faith, salvation, or redemption? Questions about the 'object'
pole in the process of knowing or understanding are no more
straightforward. In principle, if human perceptions can ever
be true, the structures and order which seem to be presup-
posed in processes of understanding are potentially given and
not merely imposed arbitrarily on *the given* by the human
mind. We may acknowledge, with Kant, the active part
played by the mind in selecting, shaping, and ordering what is
thought to count as the raw data of human observation and
experience. But that the whole process is even *capable of
resulting* in rational understanding of the given might be said
to depend, from the standpoint of Christian belief, on the
prior presence and activity of God as Creator Spirit. In the
biblical traditions creation is seen as an establishing of an
ordered reality. Its elements can be 'separated', and are sufficiently stable to be intelligibly articulated in language through
bearing names (Gen. 1.3ff.). All this stands in contrast to

what would otherwise be 'formless void' (Hebrew, *tohu wa-bohu,* Gen 1.2; cf Is. 45.18). The empty, featureless waste exhibits nothing identifiable, let alone ordered, which might become an object of thought. With the hindsight of Christian revelation, and as a piece of speculative theology, it might be said that the very thinkableness of the universe finds its ground in the creative work of God's Spirit.

This kind of approach however, has taken us far from the centre of biblical language about the Spirit and truth. The biblical writers are more than cautious about speaking of God's Spirit as that which immanently pervades the world. Indeed Paul seems to correct the idea of an immanent cosmic spirit similar to that found in contemporary Stoic philosophy when he declares, 'No one comprehends the thoughts of God except the Spirit of God. Now we have received not the spirit of the world but the Spirit which is from (Greek, *ek;* in effect 'who proceeds from') God, that we might understand the gifts bestowed on us by God' (1 Cor. 2.11 ff.). To be sure, Paul closely associates the work of the Holy Spirit with that which is rational and ordered. Prophecy inspired by the Spirit does not entail suspension of mental activity and conscious assessment (1 Cor. 14.13ff.). He regrets that the Galatians have been 'bewitched' into attitudes in which their minds have not been active (Gal.3.1, Greek *anoētoi*). The mind (Greek, *nous*) is to be renewed (Rom.12.2). Paul could never have agreed with his Jewish contemporary Philo, that 'the mind is evicted at the arrival of the divine Spirit, but when he departs the mind returns to its tenancy' (Philo, *Who is the Heir of Divine Things?* 53:265). Nevertheless, if the Bible speaks at all of the ground of potential rationality in the cosmos, the biblical traditions ascribe this to God's Wisdom or to God's Word, or even to the cosmic Christ, rather than to the Holy Spirit.

The Wisdom literature embodies this tradition firmly. Wisdom is protrayed as declaring: 'When he established the heavens, I was there, when he drew a circle on the face of the deep, when he made firm the skies above ... when he assigned to the sea its limit ... then I was beside him, like a master workman...' (Proverbs 8.27ff.). In the gospel of John, it is the Word (Greek, *logos*) who is 'with God' in the beginning, without whom nothing created was made (1.1ff.). It is in the *Logos,* rather than in the Spirit, that 'all things hold together' in potential system or intelligible order (Col.1.17). The meaning of the difficult verse in Ephesians containing the word sometimes translated 'unite all things' (RSV, Greek *anakephalaiō*) is probably that God purposed to bring everything 'to a coherent focus in Christ' (Eph. 1.10).

The actual phrase 'the Spirit of truth' belongs most characteristically to the writings of John in the New Testament, although it also occurs in Jewish literature of the time including the Dead Sea Scrolls. Both the First Epistle of John and the *Rule of the Community* (among the Dead Sea Scrolls) draw a contrast between 'the spirit of truth' and the 'spirit of error' (1 John 4.6; Rule [= 1QS] 3:17ff.; cf. Testament of Judah 20.1). Here the reference is broad. What is at issue in 1 John is that all claims to be 'inspired' should be submitted to examination and tested. It is not certain that 'spirit' refers to the Spirit of God, although it may well do so. The Johannine gospel clearly refers to the Spirit of God whom John also calls the 'Paraclete' in the final discourses, but the notion of truth which occurs in this context is also more specific. The direction of thought in these discussions makes it beyond doubt that the well-known promise 'The Spirit of truth ... will guide you into all (the?) truth' (John 16.13) does not in its original context deal with the human quest for truth in general terms at all. Rather it promises trustworthy guidance to the Christian community for the task of understanding Christ and the implications of the gospel message.

Other passages in the fourth gospel confirm this impression. The first reference to 'the Spirit of truth' in these discourses underlines the role of the Holy Spirit in continuing the ministry of Christ and his disclosure of the gospel. It is said that the world cannot receive him, in the sense that the world's openness to receive this Spirit reflects its measure of openness to the message of Christ (14.16ff). The coming of the Spirit fulfils Christ's promise, 'I will come to you' (v.18). 'The Spirit of truth, who proceeds from the Father, will bear witness to me' (15.26). This truth is said elsewhere in the Gospel of John to bring freedom (8.32). But here grace also entails judgement. For whereas in other religious writings light offers general illumination of the human mind, in John light shows up everything to be what it is, in an exposure which thereby brings judgement. 'This is the judgement, that the light has come into the world, and men loved darkness rather than light...' (3.19). Illusion about oneself, about the world, and about Christ, John affirms, may be initially more comfortable and therefore, for many, desirable.

The healing of an unsighted person now becomes a model or symbol of Christ's concern for those who cannot (or will not) 'see'. The healing narrative (9.1ff.) is set in a context of discourse which begins with the words of Jesus 'I am the light of the world' (8.1); includes the personal testimony 'one thing I know, that though I was blind, now I see' (9.25); and concludes with the judgement: 'If you were blind you would have no guilt, but now that you say, "We see", your guilt remains' (9.41).

After Jesus has completed his earthly witness and ministry, the Spirit of truth will continue this work of exposure and disclosure. 'He will convince the world of sin and of righteousness and of judgement' (16.8). The Spirit will press home those verdicts which will become publicly definitive only at the last judgement. Meanwhile, before that time, this work of the Spirit remains more akin to that of a therapist than a prosecutor or judge. He exposes that which needs attention, so that life can then be grounded in reality rather than in illusion, or self-deception, or other people's subjective opinion. The contrast between judgements which reflect the truth of God and the seductiveness or fickleness of 'what other people think' becomes a major theme in John's gospel: 'How can you believe, who receive approval (RSV glory) from one another, and do not seek the approval (RSV glory) that comes from the only God?' (5.44). 'They loved the praise of men more than the praise of God' (12.43). By contrast, Jesus declares, 'I am the way, and the truth, and the life... He who has seen me has seen the Father' (14.6,9). The Holy Spirit continues the witness after the resurrection.

It would be a mistake, however, to conclude from these initial observations that a theology of the Holy Spirit addresses only narrower questions about truth as the truth of the Christian message. As we shall shortly see, even in the New Testament conceptions of truth are neither uniform nor naive. But before we can explore these issues further, we need first to clarify more sharply what we mean by 'true' and 'truth' in the wider context of more philosophical discussion.

WHAT IS TRUTH? SOME APPROACHES AND MODELS

Perhaps the most widely assumed model of truth is that which has come to be known as the *correspondence* theory. If we ask whether some oral news or newspaper report is true, we are asking whether the statements in question *correspond* with the actual states of affairs which they portray. False statements are those which fail to correspond with what is the case. Aristotle in philosophy and Thomas Aquinas in theology advocated this approach to an understanding of truth.

In common with all the major theories of truth, this approach helps us with some problems and in some contexts, but cannot address others. It operates in everyday life where we have some means of independent access to the state of affairs behind the statements which we wish to assess. Independent witnesses may verify or disconfirm the oral news or newspaper report as true or false. But sometimes we do not have independent access of this kind. Questions about historical occurrences in the ancient world, or about ultimate issues in philosophy or theology do not easily fall into this pattern. A problem of circularity can arise. To borrow a well-known philosophical simile, it is like buying a second copy of the same newspaper to verify whether what the first copy said was true. At the level of a theory of reality, or of a belief-system, the model seems to make sense, just as it makes sense as model in everyday life. But its cash value concretely for the enquirer is more problematic. Indeed even more everyday examples are not immune from difficulty. When a cartographer seeks to portray a true picture of the world by means of a map, the correspondence between the paper and the terrain rests not only on conventions of depiction but also on value judgements about what is most important in the enterprise. For various systems of projection can be chosen to portray three-dimensional reality on two-dimensional paper. One will convey truth about surface area; another truth about latitudes; another, truth about routes and distances. Truth, even for the correspondence theory, transcends flat description alone.

In historical enquiries, where direct or independent access to events can no longer be gained, correspondence models begin to give ground to questions about coherence or consistency of witnesses and sources. When we move from the appeal to experience (the empirical tradition), to the operation of mathematics and logic (the rationalist tradition), we move to a second model of truth, namely the *coherence* theory. A mathematical proposition is 'true' if it *coheres* with other propositions within the system. Logical consistency becomes the key criterion of truth. In the history of ideas, Leibniz, Spinoza, and Hegel expounded and advocated this approach.

Like the correspondence theory, the coherence theory of truth assists us in exposing falsehoods. Tests of consistency not only sharpen thinking but dispel illusion. Its limitations begin to come to light when we ask how much can be accounted for, or even described, within the same single system. It is possible to have self-contained systems in logic, in theology, or in mathematics which do not engage with the historical realities of human life. Further, we find that as disclosure, discovery, history and experience advance, either more than one system emerges, or the system becomes flexible, open-ended, and capable of embodying novelty. In the philosophy of science, the well-worn example is that of the electron which, in some respects, is to be seen as a particle; and in other respects, is to be seen as a wave. We traced some of the implications of this for an understanding of truth in the sciences and in theology in our previous report, *We Believe in God*. It is possible to have a self-consistent system of propositions gathered round an axiom which bears no relation to the reality of the world (other than a semiotic or linguistic one). It is equally possible that reality transcends what can be expressed within a single system.

Faced by such difficulties, some philosophers have resorted to a third model of truth. Truth proves itself to be what it is only by its production of constructive consequences. In its crudest form, this is the *pragmatic* model of truth. An engineer discovers whether a calculation or assumption was true by whether it *works*. C. S. Peirce argued that truth would emerge as what it was in the long run. Truth is the eventual outcome of enquiry. William James related truth to behaviour. Recently this kind of approach has been refined to a highly sophisticated level by Richard Rorty and others who reject any notion of truth in philosophy as a kind of 'mirror' of reality. Rorty entitled his major book *Philosophy and the Mirror of Nature*. The only possible criterion of truth, he argues, is whether it 'edifies'. This is not moral or religious edification, but the ability to take the next step, in a chain of enquiry, in a direction which cannot yet be specified.

The force of this approach is considerable. Falsehood and self-deception lead us into blind alleys and bring us to a halt. Jesus told his disciples, 'You will know them by their fruits' (Matt. 7.16). Gamaliel advised the court that if Christian claims were false, they would come to nothing, but if they were true, 'you will not be able to overthrow them' (Acts 5.39). But how long do we have to wait before we can see whether progress is permanent? More sharply, what counts as progress or success? Have not illusions captured the minds of thousands, if not millions, and led them on (in both senses of the phrase) towards what they perceived as success? Once again, this model makes its own contribution to the subject but it becomes seductive and anti-self-critical if it is regarded as a comprehensive theory of truth.

Another group of philosophers is quick to point out that in everyday life we utter the words 'It is true' more often, as an exclamation than as a statement. What does it add to the statement 'Smith is a good dentist' to say 'It is true that Smith is a good dentist'? The words often serve as a commentary on the stance of the speaker, or a commentary on the statement itself. A. Tarski, stressing the latter, offered a *semantic* theory of truth. P. F. Strawson, stressing the former, called attention to the self-involving character of truth claims for the speaker. His model represents a *performative* theory of truth, and develops the work of Austin. To say 'It is true that Smith is a good dentist' is both to make a statement about Smith and to add a personal recommendation, probably on the basis of first-hand experience.

These models, too, like the others, make a contribution to our understanding of truth. Certainly the performative model accords with research in New Testament studies into the nature of early Christian credal confessions. To confess Christ as Lord in the New Testament community was both to make a truth claim about the exaltation and vindication of Christ, *and* to nail one's own colours to the mast as one who belonged to Christ as his servant or his slave. True confession at this level is prompted by the Holy Spirit. 'No one can say "Jesus is Lord" except by the Holy Spirit' (1 Cor.12.3). Apprehending truth and having a personal stake in it are both involved.

We cannot attempt to offer an exhaustive list of possible models of truth. The four or five approaches which we have examined represent the main ones. Our next step is to note that in the biblical writings and in Christian tradition all these models have some part to play. We may then consider further questions about the role of the Holy Spirit.

TRUTH IN THOUGHT, WORD, DEED AND LIFE

From between the end of the nineteenth century until after the middle of the twentieth, it was customary, almost conventional, for many biblical scholars to make sweeping claims about the difference between 'Hebrew' and 'Greek' views of truth. In an over-simple scheme of dialectic, it was alleged that the 'Hebraic' notion of truth was fundamentally practical; the Greek view generally theoretical; and the New Testament a synthesis which combined elements from each. Supposedly the Hebrews, largely on the ground that the Hebrew word for 'truth' (*'emeth*) could also mean faithfulness, tended to equate truth with reliability. The Greeks, by contrast, were thought to have adopted a more theoretical approach. Plato held something very like both correspondence and coherence theories of truth; Protagoras and the Sophists held a more relativist view; the Sceptics maintained in theory a suspense of judgement; and all together were somehow perceived as representing 'Greek' thought.

Such a portrait of this part of the ancient world, however, is little better than a caricature. Many Greeks were not philosophers at all, and some Hebrews, as well as many Jews in later Judaism, reflected on issues more ultimate than the next practical matter. What mainly gave rise to this simplistic portrait was not only a semantic accident in the case of *'emeth,* but also the fact that the *contexts in which* Hebrew utterances about truth happen to be recorded are most frequently practical religious ones, while the *contexts in which* the word *alētheia,* truth, occurs most frequently in Greek literature happen to be philosophical ones. But there are instances of a plurality of understandings of truth within the Old Testament, within Greek literature, in Paul, in John, and in the rest of the New Testament. This should not surprise us: any *one* model of truth remains appropriate only to certain contexts of life and thought.

In the New Testament and in later Christian tradition, truth concerns thought, word, deed, life, and character. It relates to witness, to revelation, and to being anchored in reality. Paul and John certainly presuppose what we should nowadays call a correspondence model of truth when they are addressing questions about truth in speech. Paul disowns attempts to use guile, or to present false claims; his intention is to communicate truth in a straightforward way (2.Cor.4.2; 6.7; 7.14). The ethics of truthful speech is enjoined in Ephesians (4.25). In John, the Samaritan woman tells the truth about her marital status (4.18), and the Baptist speaks truth about Jesus (10.41). But at a fundamental level, reality can be masked. Paul shares with the preachers of the Jewish synagogues the Jewish-Christian convention that pagan religion and morals lead to suppression of the truth (Rom. 1.18 ff.; cf. Wis. 13.1ff., 14.8ff.). Truth, for Paul, becomes sharply focused as the content of the gospel message (Gal.2.5; cf 2 Thess.2.13).

John takes up the contrast, by implication, between appearance and reality. Israel has been chosen as God's vine, but Israel's history proved this to be more apparent than real. By contrast, Jesus Christ is 'the real vine' (15.1). Some set great store on Moses' giving manna to Israel, and this coloured their expectations of the Messiah. But Christ's own flesh, which he gives, is a 'real' food indeed (6.55). Worship is sometimes only a show arising from human religiosity and aspiration. But worship prompted by the Spirit is 'real' (4.23.f.). John has a special interest in witness. Human witnesses like the Baptist and the Samaritan woman testify to Jesus, and God's own witness is said to be added. 'True' witness is reliable, and dependable witnesses speak truth as they see it (8.13ff.). But truth, in John, always touches life as well as thought or word. Hence, probably against the background of Exodus 34, Jesus Christ as the Word-made-flesh reveals in his enfleshed person the actuality of God, 'full of grace and truth' (1.14).

What is the role of the Holy Spirit in all this? First, if Christ definitively discloses the heart of God in his enfleshed person, the Holy Spirit is said to continue this work of disclosure. The process of revelation which takes place during the ministry of Jesus both continues what was begun in the Old Testament and looks forward to clearer future disclosure. In the present there is a dimension of hiddenness. This is acknowledged. When he dons the servant's apron, Jesus tells Peter: 'What I am doing you do not know now, but afterward you will understand' (John 13.7). 'The Spirit of truth, who proceeds from the Father, will bear witness to me' (15.26). The First Epistle of John develops the same theme. After speaking of the Christian confession of Jesus as God's authentic self-disclosure, the writer continues: 'And the Spirit is the witness, because the Spirit is the truth' (1 John 5.7). It is important for the writer that this witness transcends mere human conviction or opinion (5.8ff.). As in Paul, 'it is the Spirit himself bearing witness with our spirit that we are children of God' (Rom. 8.16; cf. Gal. 4.6). Even in Hebrews, where reference to the Holy Spirit is rare, the Holy Spirit 'bears witness to us' (Heb. 10.15). In the Revelation of John, the message is a prophecy, a disclosure, and a testimony (Rev. 1.1ff.; 22.6f., 16). But here an invitation to personal experience and appropriation is offered to all who sigh for what is so far beyond their grasp; 'the Spirit and the Bride say "Come" … Let him who is thirsty, come…' (Rev.22.17).

The truth disclosed through the presence and work of the Spirit, therefore, concerns what we earlier described as the two poles of the subject and object. Kierkegaard argued that truth cannot be reduced to what can be blandly packaged and accepted on a plate. Without genuine subjective appropriation, without perhaps conflict and struggle, certainly without change and transformation, certain kinds of truth cannot be perceived. Without such appropriation and change 'truth becomes untruth in this or that person's mouth', we turn Christian truth into 'what is its exact opposite', and then 'thank God for the great and inestimable privilege of being a Christian' (S.Kierkegaard, *Attack on 'Christendom'*, p. 150).

Kierkegaard echoes the words of Jesus in John that the truth is inseparable from the way and the life (John 14.6). 'Everyone who has a result merely as such does not possess it, for he has not the *way*' (Kierkegaard, *The Concept of Irony*, p. 340). Truth, in this context, is not merely subjective; but it does involve human subjectivity. The New Testament writers did not possess this particular terminological tool. But they could declare: 'God's love has been poured into our hearts through the Holy Spirit which has been given to us' (Rom.5.5).

The dimension which is entirely missing from Kierkegaard's otherwise helpful emphasis is the corporate one. Truth emerges not only in the conflicts and struggles of the individual, but also in the conflicts and struggles of the believing community. This is what we should expect not only when we reflect on the Church's history, but also when we recall the point made elsewhere in this volume that the Holy Spirit is given corporately to the community of God's people as 'shareholders' in the common gift (Greek *koinōnia* of the Spirit; fellowship of the Spirit in the sense of that which we share, 2 Cor.13.14). The performative model of truth remains a contributory element: the community consists of those who are making a stand, who have a personal stake in the commonality which they share. But they are also a corroborative community. Each affirms and confirms the witness of the other to the reality of God and to the truth of the gospel. Each may also interact with others in comparing and contrasting different partial understandings which arise from the fragmentary perceptions of individuals.

This is the way in which the Spirit of truth guides the community 'into all the truth' (John 16.13). On the analogy of Paul's assertions about the sharing of the Spirit's gifts among the community, it would be unlikely that any single individual would have a monopoly of this truth. Believers and seekers need one another. 'Iron sharpens iron, and one man sharpens another' (Prov.27.17). The conflicts at Corinth between the weak and the strong, or between the better off and the poor, sharpened understandings of the relation between knowledge, freedom, and love, and led to a formulation of a theology of the Lord's Supper in 1 Corinthians. Clashes between what amounted to cliques at Corinth led to deeper reflection about the nature of the ministry and of the relation between 'wisdom' and the cross. Struggles with Judaizing influences, or perhaps with the respective status of Jewish and Gentile Christians, led to Paul's more sharply articulating the truth of justification by grace alone through faith. Marcion's rejection of the Old Testament helped the second-century Church to appreciate its value as part of the one revelation of the one God.

All this bears some relation to the *pragmatic* model of truth. The people of God learn as they walk. Discipleship is a journey and a pilgrimage in which we never cease to be learners. All knowledge is subject to correction as we proceed. In the report *We Believe in God* we acknowledged this, and we argued that this did not make existing knowledge unreliable or inadequate for the task. The disclosures of the ever-present Spirit are for the practical purpose of 'building up' a community into Christian maturity over a process, not a single event, of growth (1 Cor.12.7; 14.3,5; cf. Eph.4.11ff.). The measure of 'maturity' is 'the stature of the fulness of Christ' (Eph.4.13). It is also, as we have seen, a matter of personally taking a stand; of being a witness and a partaker (1 Pet.5.1). To declare, with Luther, 'Here I stand', is part of what is meant by Christian confession of faith. When they are put on trial before hostile accusers or courts of enquiry, Christians must be prepared to give an account of their faith (1 Pet.3.15). But Jesus tells his disciples not to be anxious about what they are to say: 'For it is not you who speak, but the Holy Spirit' (Mk. 13.11; cf Matt.10.20). Putting oneself personally on the line belongs, once again, to the performative conception of truth. Yet none of this, we noted, is thought to arise merely through personal decision. We examined a number of those passages in Paul and especially in John which ground statements about Christ (or about the self and the world) in a reality which is neither illusory nor merely apparent, even if public verification of this will not emerge fully until the end of history. Paul himself acknowledges the provisional nature of all human judgements: 'Do not pronounce judgement before the time, before the Lord comes, who will bring to light the things now hidden' (1 Cor.4.5). 'Now I know in part; then I shall understand fully' (1 Cor.13.12).

COHERENCE, INSPIRATION AND ULTIMACY

In spite of the importance and relevance of the performance and pragmatic models of truth, Christian claims about truth disclosed in and by the work of the Holy Spirit clearly go beyond these areas. Truth is not simply autobiography, or autobiographical testimony about what seems to 'work'. Philosophers have called attention to the intellectual vulnerability of the kind of perception which can be traced from C. S. Peirce and John Dewey to Richard Rorty, as well as the kind of standpoint reflected in Jacquer Derrida's poststructuralism where truth has been reduced, in effect, to 'how it is with me'. In a pragmatic and pluralistic culture the Christian Church may also be tempted to lose its intellectual or rational nerve and to retreat into performative or functional attitudes towards truth, in which biography or autobiography, corporate or individual, becomes the order of the day. The renewal movement has encouraged a new emphasis on narrative testimony, and this carries with it some particular strengths and weaknesses. Biography and autobiography, whether on the part of individuals or groups, can be warm and living, and it is a fundamental part of performative Christian testimony, as we earlier observed. But pragmatic and performative models need to be supplemented and tested through other ways of assessment, if the claims of Christians about reality and ultimacy are to be taken seriously. There can be multiple explanations for what 'works': a *variety* of causes may give rise to a sense of liberation from anxiety or from guilt; to an experience of change and transformation; to the enjoyment of worship; to an enhanced vitality, power, or ability to cope. The Holy Spirit may well be at work here, but not necessarily in every case.

Josephine Bax calls our attention in this context of renewal to the importance of the challenge of crisis being 'strong enough to bring about a change of direction, but not so strong as to reduce us to despair' (*The Good Wine: Spiritual Renewal in the Church of England,* p.33). But, as Karl Jaspers the philosopher emphasized in these boundary situations or limit situations, what is perceived as the truth may take a variety of forms. It is truth *for the person concerned.* In keeping with his own existentialist horizons, Jaspers refused to identify this existential truth with anything given, and certainly not with the message of the gospel of Christ. Indeed his definition of truth is turned virtually the other way round: it is 'whatever I find' when the masks have been removed. But Jaspers also acknowledged that different people find different things when this cannot happen. It remains, at best, an existentialist view of truth.

Christian truth claims certainly embody and embrace this performative or existential dimension of narrative testimony, but they can never be entirely reduced to it. For *ultimacy* cannot be defined in terms of human need and experience. The Holy Spirit is not simply a mythological projection of the human spirit, but a ground beneath and beyond it. We must look further at other models of truth.

The coherence model has so far received less attention than others in the present discussion. Yet in some respects it is the most suggestive of all the models in the context of claims about ultimate truth. The most serious problem about this model, we noted, arose from the incompleteness of any system when truth viewed from within that system was related to human life, or to God. In the biblical writings, however, symbols and images of ultimacy are more usually temporal rather than spiritual. We observed Paul's contrast, for example, between the hiddenness and ambiguity of the 'now' and definitive public knowledge which God will disclose 'then'. The logical grammar of the 'last judgement' is that it is understood to represent a definitive pronouncement, at the close of history, which cannot be revised. It will publicly corroborate, or in some cases disconfirm provisional knowledge, values, or truth claims which hitherto could only be assumed or grasped in faith. In the present, in Paul's words, 'we walk by faith, not by sight' (2 Cor. 5.7). But, he continues, there will come a decisive moment when all will be made clear (5.10). John Hick takes up this principle in the context of logical positivism and calls it the principle of 'eschatological verification'. In the context of a different philosophical tradition, Wolfhart Pannenberg develops the idea in relation to Hegel's claim that truth emerges definitively or absolutely only in the context of the whole.

If we can entertain this approach seriously, even at least as an intelligible hypothesis which deserves attention, this has implications for a theology of the Holy Spirit and the work of the Spirit in the present and the future. In his book *Christ and Time* Oscar Cullmann, drawing on insights from the New Testament, particularly from Paul's epistles, describes the Holy Spirit as 'the anticipation of the end in the present' (p.72). Verdicts and disclosures, which are capable of public access and confirmation only in the future, are now already brought home convincingly to the believing heart or to the open mind. This is the thrust of the material about the Paraclete in John which we have already noted. The Spirit, as it were, anticipates disclosures which in principle belong to the last judgement (John 16.7ff.). Because history is not yet complete, our perceptions and judgements remain hidden. We see edges of God's ways, but we still await the sifting through of ambiguities and the full revelation of God's glory. Nevertheless, the axiom around which the whole growing system revolves has already been disclosed in advance: 'He who has seen me has seen the Father' (John 14.9). 'God ... has spoken by a Son ... he ... bears the very stamp of his nature' (Heb.1.2f.). 'When the Spirit of truth comes ... he will declare to you the things that are to come. He will glorify me, for he will take what is mine and declare it to you' (John 16.13f.).

This perspective holds together a number of beliefs which most Christians will wish simultaneously to affirm. It holds together the unity of truth as that which concerns all reality with the particularity of the definitive disclosure of God in Christ. It holds together an acknowledgment that the present is marked by ambiguities in which God sometimes remains hidden, with a confidence that faith, in the context of this hiddenness, will be vindicated and confirmed. It holds together the recognition that while the performative and pragmatic dimensions of truth remain important, truth claims also concern, for the Christian, matters of ultimate reality.

Two more areas invite consideration before we conclude. The first concerns the Christian tradition that the Holy Spirit has uniquely inspired the revelation of God in scripture; the second concerns the relation between continuity and novelty in the Holy Spirit's work of disclosing truth.

One of the fundamental beliefs expressed in the historic creeds is that the Holy Spirit 'has spoken through the prophets'. The phrase echoes the language of 2 Peter, where the prophets are said to have spoken as they were 'carried along' (Greek *pheromenoi,* Vulgate *inspirati*) by the Holy Spirit (2 Pet.1.21). Similarly in 2 Timothy the Greek phrase 'inspired by God' *(theopneustos)* is rendered *divinitus inspirata* in the Latin versions (2. Tim. 3.16).

In the early centuries, indeed up to relatively modern times, the Church seemed to speak with one voice about the Holy Spirit's inspiration of the Bible. In response to Marcion's attempt to drive a wedge between the Old and the New Testaments, the Church of the second and third centuries affirmed that the same Holy Spirit inspired both sets of writings. Nicene Catholics re-affirmed the principle in the fourth century. Cyril of Jerusalem asserts, 'There is one Holy Spirit who preached Christ through the prophets ... let no one therefore divide the Old Testament from the New; let no one say that the Spirit in the Old Testament is one, and the Spirit in the New Testament is another' *(Catecheses* 16.4). In general, the Church Fathers regarded the biblical writings as the writings of the Holy Spirit. The biblical authors were, in effect, the Spirit's tool and mouthpiece. The Church had taken over the view of biblical inspiration which could be found in rabbinic Judaism and included the New Testament as well as the Old within this framework.

In modern times however, a more complex account of the nature of biblical inspiration is called for. As J. T. Burtchaell comments by way of summary of modern discussion, 'The real issue here is what confounds scholars in so many areas: the manner in which individual human events are jointly caused by both God and man' (*Catholic Theories of Biblical Inspiration Since 1910*, p.279). There are both intellectual reasons and theological reasons to do with religious devotion why we should be reluctant either to devalue or to overrate what is involved in 'inspiration'. If we minimise the part played by human agency and personality, we run the risk of idolatry, by elevating human words to the status of the wholly divine. On the other hand, if we underestimate the agency of the Holy Spirit, we risk losing sight of the givenness of the biblical writings as that which addresses us from beyond ourselves with a saving and authentic word. As James Smart has observed, while it was a genuine achievement of modern biblical scholarship to establish the human character of the biblical writings, this emphasis should not become so obsessional that it eclipses their status or function as genuinely expressing a message from God. The Roman Catholic writer Bruce Vawter attempts to hold the two dimensions together. He writes, 'Often enough they (the prophets) insisted that the thoughts to which they gave words were not of their own devising, that they spoke them in obedience to a superior moral will ... that at times they would even have preferred to leave them unsaid... It is equally obvious that these thoughts had also passed through the prophets' own minds' (*Biblical Inspiration*, p.17).

Such comments take us forward, but they also leave difficulties. It is at this point that it may be helpful to return to an earlier consideration about the Holy Spirit and truth. For narrower questions about the Spirit and 'inspiration' (especially the inspiration of the Bible) need to be placed in a broader theological context. Four principles emerge. First, the Holy Spirit comes as one who is beyond, and yet also within. There is therefore a givenness about the Spirit's disclosure of truth which goes beyond purely human explanation or purely human discovery. Second, the Spirit does not operate independently of God's words and deeds in Christ, or in the history of Israel. There is continuity of identity in this work or witness which enables John to assert that the Spirit witnesses to Christ; that he is sent by God 'in Christ's name', or that he will 'bring to your remembrance' the words of Christ (John 14.26; cf.16.7ff.). Similarly Paul understands the disclosure and transformation that comes through the Holy Spirit as 'having the mind of Christ' (1 Cor.2. 12ff.). Third, the work of the Holy Spirit makes it possible not only to perceive truth but also to appropriate truth and to live it out. While the witness of the Spirit may point to words spoken or to deeds done in the past, the focus of the witness concerns present attitudes, assessments, and actions. Through the witness of the Spirit, even the past comes alive for the present. Fourth, all these factors operate in relation to given purposes. The truth disclosed through the Spirit serves goals of human change and growth, of transformation of life and obedient service of God and of others. Bezalel's gift of craftsmanship, for example, or the Judges' gifts of administration, served particular purposes for the communities which they served.

When Christians sometimes speak, therefore, of the Spirit's witnessing to the truth or to the reality of the Christian message of the cross, what is at issue is not simply or primarily the possession of a set of facts about the crucifixion of Jesus of Nazareth, but an understanding and appropriation of Christ's death and resurrection as somehow being also my death and my resurrection in the present. The Holy Spirit is said, for example, to apply the objective truth that in Christ human persons may become children of God at the level of a subjective awareness and experience: 'Because you are sons, God has sent

the Spirit of his Son into our hearts crying "Abba! Father!"'
(Gal.4.6).

In the same way, discussions about the nature of 'inspiration' usually operate on at least two different levels. One level
concerns continuity, or internal coherence, between the givenness of a past which includes the founding events of the
Christian faith, and lived experience in the present. In this
respect James Barr has pointed out that involvement with the
Bible is integral too in being a Christian; 'It is believing in a
particular God, the God who has manifested himself in a way
that has some sort of unique and specific expression in the
Bible' (*Explorations in Theology* 7, p.52). On the other hand at
a different level claims about 'Inspiration' are also located
firmly in the present. Following the tradition of the
Reformers, Norman Snaith observes, 'The authority of the
Bible ... for me ... rests in the inner witness of the Holy
Spirit' (*The Inspiration and Authority of the Bible,* p.45).
Through the testimony of the Spirit, John Calvin writes, the
scriptures ring true 'by God's own witness' (*Institutes* 1.7.5).

Questions about the inspiration of the Holy Spirit, then,
especially in relation to the Bible, can best be approached
within the framework of broader concerns about the Spirit
and truth. The focus of such questions is such that they involve the present no less than the past; action, no less than
knowledge; transformation, no less than the acquisition of
understanding. To ask 'truth, for what?' is not necessarily to
compartmentalize theories of truth into different areas such as
truths of science and truths of religion. It is simply to
recognize that the truth which is disclosed through the Holy
Spirit concerns more than knowledge about certain states of
affairs. It entails the gift of an angle of vision, or the apprehension of a frame of reference, which affects not only what is
perceived but also the one who perceives. The emergence of
the canon of scripture in the life of the early Church calls to
mind the performative and semantic models of truth. The
Church said, in effect 'This is where we stand. *This* is where
we hear the witness of the Spirit'.

Finally, the coherence model of truth underlines an implication for questions about continuity and novelty. It is understandable that in the renewal movement attention should be paid to the element of change, transformation, newness, novelty, or even surprise which accompanies what is perceived as the work of the Holy Spirit. This is not contrary to the nature of the Spirit. For the Spirit remains sovereign creator, transcendent and holy, who bursts through all human systems of thought and practice. We cannot manipulate the Spirit's presence and blessing, for the Spirit can be like the wind, which 'blows where it wills' (John 3.8). All the same, the Holy Spirit does not undermine the Spirit's own work. What is disclosed by the Spirit of truth coheres with the revelation of the word of Christ and the apostolic witness to the gospel of the cross. The criterion of coherence is implicitly built into the New Testament injunctions about testing (1 John 4.2f.; 5.1ff.). Even if systems are expanded and transcended by the Spirit's disclosures, later revelation will not contradict earlier witness, and it will cohere with what remains in principle the central axiom of Christ and the cross.

8

The Spirit and Creation

The discussion of the Spirit of Truth in the preceding chapter leads easily and naturally to a consideration of some of the scientific truth into which we have been led. We start from the realization that any account of human existence which recognizes its meaning and purpose will have to take account (in Kant's convenient phrase) both of the 'moral law within' and of the 'starry heavens above'. The interior and exterior aspects of our experience are not two separate and disparate enterprises, disjoined from each other by a division running between a public world of fact and a private world of value. There is but one world in which the Spirit is at work, inspiring and energising. An existentialist theology, concerned only with the human psyche, is too narrowly confined. It fails to take account of the fact that that psyche emerged within the evolving process of the world. What God made together we separate at our peril.

In consequence, an inquiry into the nature and working of the Holy Spirit will have to include an inquiry into the nature and working of the physical world. We are what we are because of our past and the consideration of that past takes us back not simply to our birth and childhood, nor to the first stirrings of our culture, nor even just to the origin of biological life, but to the very beginning of all things in the origin of the universe itself. When we lift our eyes from ourselves to take in the significance of the cosmos, our discernment of the Holy Spirit will be not only through an aesthetic appreciation of the wonders of the world, but also through an intellectual understanding of that world, gained through the natural sciences.

Both science and religion spring from the same roots of

puzzlement, wonder and the desire to understand. Science, it is often said, tends to ask 'how' questions whilst religion asks 'why' questions. One seeks mechanism (understood as whatever physical way things come to be, not simply the mechanical); the other seeks meaning. Quite so sharp a separation is too crude a characterization, for mechanism must be understood if meanings are rightly to be discerned. Theology must take natural science into account; the theologians need to do their scientific homework. Neglect of it may have contributed to modern feelings of the irrelevance of religion.

We welcome science's discoveries about the world. To the extent that scientists are searching for the truth (and that is the motivation of all fundamental scientific inquiry), we are glad to make common cause with them. For us today, the promise that the Spirit leads us into all truth must certainly be understood to include the truth of science. Our purpose is to argue for the widest possible context in which to do theology. Religious doctrine must take account of the history of the physical world as the setting for the history of humanity and also as the story of God's universal creative activity. Needless to say, the latter is understood as the continuous sustaining of an evolving process and not, in a deistic way, as merely an instant of initiation.

The Bible begins with creation stories expressed in terms of the cosmologies of their day. It must surely be our purpose to make similar use of the vastly better informed cosmology, now available to us. Other sources of creation theology in the Old Testament include Second Isaiah (perhaps influenced by contact with the astronomically quite sophisticated culture of Babylon) and the Wisdom writers (who in their cool appraisal of the world around them represent the nearest that ancient Israel got to a 'scientific' tradition). The prologue of John's Gospel relates the creation of all things to the action of the *Logos*. One of the concepts constellated around the Word is that of rational order. There is, therefore, encouragement from 'the book of scripture' to attempt to read 'the book of nature' with all due seriousness.

Science has an impressive story to tell about cosmic history. In brief we may say that just as man emerged through biological evolution, so the earth emerged from the ashes of dead stars, which in their turn emerged from the hydrogen and helium formed in the first three minutes of the universe's history, a history which in the shortest instants following on the fiery explosion of the Big Bang (if we are to believe the boldest speculations of the cosmologists) had already seen a sequence of remarkable transformations in the nature of cosmic actuality. Cosmologists are able to attempt to speak of the universe when it was only a fraction of a second old because it was then so simple and undifferentiated in its structure – at one stage an almost uniform energetic soup of elementary particles, for instance. Yet, over a fifteen-billion-year history, that initial simplicity has evolved systems as complex and interesting as ourselves. Out of stardust has come humankind, beings capable of selfconsciousness and spiritual awareness. To speak thus is by no means to embrace a reductionist account. The history of cosmic evolution appears continuous. Scientific inspection reveals no need to postulate the injection of a new ingredient before humankind could come to be, but that history is open to an interpretation emphasizing the need to consider entities in their totality, within which humanity can be recognized as novel and unique. 'Mere matter' (as it might have seemed) has proved to be endowed with an astonishing degree of fruitfulness. That from the processes of the universe have emerged creatures capable of understanding the cosmos is a profound and moving mystery.

It is time to be more specific. We are seeking in this book to speak not of God in general, but more especially of the work of the Holy Spirit. And the subject of this chapter is the Spirit in relation to creation. The Spirit did not first take to the world stage at Pentecost. Nor is the Spirit's activity confined simply to those who lay claim to the Spirit. Everywhere and at all times the Spirit has been at work. How are we to think of this creative activity?

Though we are mindful of the theological tradition which

asserts that the Holy Trinity operates externally *(ad extra)* as a divine unity, it seems appropriate nevertheless to seek some characterization of what might be considered the particular mode of the work of the Spirit in creation. We recognize the Father as the fount of being, the eternal origin of all temporal existence, the ground and guarantor of the universe. The Word speaks to us of those rational principles with which the cosmos is endowed, since we have noted that such a notion of cosmic order is one of the concepts associated with the Greek *Logos,* used by John in the prologue to his gospel. There is a profound sense of wonder among those who study physical science at the rational transparency of the world – the way that realms of experience far removed from the everyday yet prove to be open in their pattern and structure to our inquiry – and the remarkable rational beauty so revealed, which exhibits itself most strikingly in the economy and elegance of the mathematical statements of fundamental physical law. The Old Testament picture of Wisdom acting as God's delighting consort in creation (to which we referred in the preceding chapter) is taken up into the New Testament's understanding of the Cosmic Christ. For the working of the Spirit we look to a meaning to be found in *paraklētos* (cf. John 14.16), namely the one alongside. What we have said about the Father and the Word has been concerned with the law and circumstances of the universe which are the given basis for cosmic process. If we are to speak of the work of the Spirit in creation, we should need to understand this work to be within that process, and the Spirit to be in relation to the evolving universe.

Immediately one senses a danger. Is the Spirit, then, to become a sophisticated version of that pseudo-deity, the God of the gaps, inserted wherever apologists could find room, as the 'explanation' of the currently inexplicable, and continually being moved on by the advance of knowledge? One must confess that not all recent Christian writing about the Spirit seems to have avoided that trap. A correction to such a tendency is provided by Bishop John V. Taylor in his book on the Spirit, *The Go-Between God* (p.28):

If we think of a Creator at all, we are to find him on the inside of creation. And if God is really on the inside, we must find him in the processes, not in the gaps. We know now that there are no gaps, no points at which a special intervention is conceivable. From first to last the process has been continuous. Nature is all of a piece, a seamless robe. There is no evidence of a break, as we once imagined, between inorganic matter and the emergence of the first living organisms; nor between man's animal precursors and the emergence of man himself. If the hand of God is to be recognised in this continuous creation, it must be found not in isolated intrusions, not in any gaps, but in the very process itself.

Our brief comments on the role of the Father and the Word in creation indicate that there is more to be said of the Creator-God (in transcendent relation to the ground of all process) than Bishop Taylor explicitly acknowledges in this passage, but we may take to heart his words as far as the role of the Spirit is concerned. The Spirit's work is certainly nothing so occasional as the word 'intervention' might seem to imply. In fact, how could God be related to creation in so fitful a way as that would suggest? There must be a continuing consistency in all that God does. It will be our contention that the process of the world is not just the inexorable unwinding of a gigantic piece of cosmic clockwork, but rather there is some flexibility to it so that a genuine becoming takes place, yielding actual novelty. In that case the possibility of some interaction between creation and the Creator-Spirit seems an appropriate expectation. We shall see in due course how the modern scientific understanding of the nature of the physical world is by no means inhospitable to this view.

One consequence of a 'God really on the inside' is that we should expect this activity to be hidden, cloaked from view by its immersion within what is going on. The Spirit's action will be subtle rather than manifest, perceptible by faith but not demonstrable by experiment. The image in Genesis 1 of 'the Spirit hovering over the waters' (if that is the correct translation) is consistent with that relationship. The hiddenness of the Spirit's activity in creation also accords with the way some Orthodox think about the nature of the divine Persons. Vladimir Lossky writes, 'The third Hypostasis of the Trinity is the only one not having His image in another Person. The Holy Spirit, as Person, remains unmanifested, hidden, concealing Himself in His very appearing'. Lossky goes on to quote St Symeon the New Theologian addressing the Spirit '...Come, hidden mystery; come, treasure without name; come, unutterable thing; ... '(*The Mystical Theology of the Eastern Church,* p. 160).

Can one whose appearance is so masked truly be spoken of as a Person? As we have noted elsewhere (pp. 34f.), it took the Church some centuries to arrive at accepting fully the divinity and personhood of the Spirit, and Christians have often subsequently found it a struggle to rise above speaking of the Spirit in terms more appropriate to an impersonal energy or influence. For many, it must be confessed, Pentecost is distinctly the least of the great festivals and it has been a benefit of the charismatic movement that it has helped to redress that balance. It is not easy to specify what personhood implies, but using 'the Christological lens' we may surely say that it must involve capacities both for action and for passion (without this exhausting the definition of personhood). W. H. Vanstone (in *The Stature of Waiting*) has drawn our attention to the way in which the verbs in the gospels relating to Christ are initially in the active but then, as the story of his earthly life draws to its close, they become predominantly passive. An account of the Spirit written only in the active voice would indeed be in danger of making the Spirit into a cosmic force, an impersonal resource of power. An account written in the passive voice alone would be the story of an impotent spectator of the world's process, a 'cosmic sponge' simply soaking up the suffering of the world. Only in a dialectic between action and passion do we discern a being whose nature calls for fitting description in personal terms. In the New Testament the Spirit is not only the source of power (e.g. Rom. 15.19) but also can be grieved (Eph. 4.30). We have to go on to ask the extent to which our experience and understanding of the physical world cohere with these theological claims for the creative work of the Spirit.

First we consider the possibility of the Spirit's *action* within the evolving process of the world. Any creative activity, bringing about that which is new, requires for its possibility that there is an openness in what is going on. Otherwise the future is just a rearrangement of what was already existing in the past, with no intrinsic novelty. In a purely mechanical universe there is no true development. Pierre Simon Laplace, the greatest of Newton's successors, conceived of a demon calculator who, knowing the present positions and velocities of all the atoms in a Newtonian world, could immediately predict the whole future and retrodict the whole past. In such a universe there would be no becoming. Time would be just an index of where one is along the tramline, not a measure of how such a universe has evolved.

There is something fishy about Laplace's picture, particularly when applied to himself. We should take with the utmost seriousness our intuition that we enjoy some room for manoeuvre within the flux of what is going on. It is a basic human experience that our futures are to some degree open. In the science of the twentieth century we have come to see that the physical world is indeed different from the way that Laplace thought about it. Partly this is due to quantum theory's abolition of precise determinism, though that is almost always only of significance for small-scale events at the atomic level or below. Much more significant for our present purpose is the fact that the theory of dynamical instabilities (the theory of chaos, as it is called) has made it plain that even Newtonian systems are far from being generally susceptible to tight prediction and control. This is due to the exquisite sensitivity that these systems display in relation to the minutest variation in their circumstance. (In a crude way this will be familiar to any snooker player!) In terms of a metaphor of Karl Popper, the universe proves to be composed of (unpredictable) clouds with only a few (predictable) clocks among them.

Laplace had supposed that his demon possessed exact knowledge of everything that is happening. It would have seemed reasonable to suppose that if that knowledge were not quite exact, then the predicted consequences would also not be quite exact, but to a degree that was contained within tolerable limits. A key discovery has been that in general this is not true. Instead, for complex dynamical systems, initial circumstances which differ from each other by only infinitesimal amounts lead to subsequent motions which diverge from each other to arbitrary degrees. One of the earliest discoveries in this area arose from the study of computer models of the weather. This is 'only half-jokingly known as the Butterfly Effect – the notion that a butterfly stirring the air today in Peking can transform storm systems next month in New York' (J. Gleick, *Chaos* p. 8). When we are concerned with systems of such delicate sensitivity, the smallest fluctuations can trigger substantial consequences.

Intrinsic unpredictability is concerned with what we can know, but it gives us unforced encouragement to go on to an option about what we believe to be the case, taking a more supple view of reality than that provided by the Laplacian straitjacket. At last a picture of the physical world is available in which there seems some degree of consonance in thinking of ourselves as among the inhabitants of that world. Its unpredictable flexibility is congruent with our experience of openness. That flexibility is not confined to living beings; the process of the universe is shot through with it. Thus there seems also the possibility for the working of the Spirit within the whole cosmic process.

It is important to be clear about what is being said. We are not claiming anything so extravagant as that the age-old problems of divine and human action are solved in detail. We simply record the death of a merely mechanical view and the birthpangs of a physics able to speak of both being *and* becoming. The openness that characterizes the modern theory of dynamical systems is due to those systems having, in their temporal development, to thread their way through a labyrinth of proliferating bifurcating possibilities. One can get some feel for what is involved by thinking of the very simplest model of a single bifurcation. Consider a bead threading a perfectly smooth wire in the shape of an inverted U. The bead rests at the top of the wire. The tiniest 'nudge' will displace it

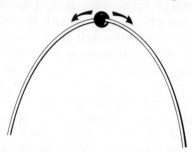

to one side or the other, and according to which way it is displaced the bead will fall either to right or to left. Thus infinitesimal triggers produce widely contrasting outcomes (way over to the right or way over to the left), in which no transaction of energy is required (the smallest displacement will do the trick if the wire is perfectly smooth).

Of course, we are concerned, not with beads on wires, but with the abstract structure of possibility illustrated by this simple system. It turns out that complex dynamical systems evolve through endless bifurcations, the negotiation of which involve zero-energy exchange but which result in non-zero difference in consequent behaviour (the bead falls to the right or to the left). This crude and simple parable may help us to consider the feasibility of the Spirit's action within the almost infinite variety and open flexibility of cosmic process. The picture is not of energetic causation (the Spirit is not an agent among other physical agencies) nor of arbitrary intervention in gaps (there is no suspension of the operation of those physical laws whose regularities the theist will see as reflections of divine faithfulness) but of a guiding within the *inherent* openness of the flux of becoming. Necessarily the Spirit's action is hidden within the cloudiness of the intrinsically unpredictable.

There is, of course, no interference with those occurrences (such as the succession of the seasons) which do enjoy a clockwork regularity. We believe that modern physical theory is entirely consonant with theological discourse of the Spirit at work 'really on the inside'.

We do not attempt to breach the hiddenness by attempting to spell out any detailed conjectures of how the Spirit has been working. A modern scientific writer has said about the universe, 'There exists alongside the entropy arrow (the direction of decay) another arrow of time, equally fundamental, and no less subtle in nature ... I refer to the fact that the universe is *progressing* – through the steady growth of structure, organisation and complexity – to ever more developed and elaborate states of matter and energy'. The writer goes on to refer to this increase in organisation as 'an objective fact' (P. Davies, *The Cosmic Blueprint*, p.20). Teilhard de Chardin called this fact complexification. The universe started extremely simple and uniform. It has become remarkably differentiated, with highly structured subsystems (such as ourselves). There is no reason to suppose that this process is not susceptible to discussion in scientific terms – indeed the quotation above is taken from a book which is about such topics as the theory of complex dynamical systems. But since science is discerning processes intrinsically open in their character, there is no reason to deny to theology the right to its own point of view, as it seeks to understand the evolving fruitfulness of the universe in terms of the patient and subtle operation of the Spirit on the inside of physical process.

The Spirit's *passion* in the creative process of the world may be most clearly discerned in relation to the suffering found within it. This thought leads us from the generalities of physics to the greater particularities of biology and ecology. The costliness and blind alleys of evolution, and the precarious environmental balances necessary for life, are part of the story of creation. The processes and organisation of human societies are indissolubly bound up with a wider economy involving other organisms and non-living components. All in the end is subject to decay. Humanity is the only member of this world known to us which is able to give voice to its continuing groans and travails as part of the waiting expectation of the ultimate glory willed by God. One of the roles of the Spirit is as the articulator of hope in the midst of passion. Because of its condemnation to futility, nature only makes ultimate sense as a creation if it is oriented towards something beyond itself. It is the Spirit who enables us to be incorporated fully into the freedom of God's redemptive act in Christ and so to know our destiny in him. United in impatient straining with the rest of the created order, we are nevertheless made by the Spirit into an earnest of that hope for liberation for which all await in eager expectation (Rom. 8.18ff.). In the Spirit we are bound to the natural world in a solidarity of pain and longing, yet we are given also in the Spirit a pledge (2 Cor.5.5.) of the final glory when we shall be incorporated, together with the whole created realm, into the life of God.

Our participation in creation is a painful thing in which the Spirit shares. Understanding the process of creation is a sacrificial task in which we share in the birthpangs of nature from suffering into hope. In our exploration of the physical world we are moved by more than just a quizzical curiosity about a work already completed. Rather, we are participating in a continuing process of which our own longings are an integral part.

This understanding gives us a renewed perception of the yearning which we believe God has had from the beginning for the completion of creation, for the Spirit lets us feel God's ceaseless love for God's own creation. This hidden action and passion together are the measure of God's generosity and steadfast love, as God freely creates the other. The Spirit's presence 'really on the inside' signifies the extent of God's renunciation and sacrifice, from whose self-giving nothing is held back. In these terms we may understand in what way the Spirit is at work 'on the inside'.

Yet the Spirit is also *at work*. This work is a continuing expression of God's tactful and steadfast relationship of gift and response to all that is, and the order and resourcefulness of creation is perceived as a corresponding response to that. Each of God's creatures is called to be faithful according to its nature, even when that means, for example, that for elements of the earth's crust their nature results in earthquakes. Hard though that saying is, it is by this acceptance of individual creaturely character that the creation glorifies its Creator (cf.Ps.148). Thus we are able to see the physical world, not only as the arena of suffering, but also as a movement of praise, that is, as a reflection back to God of God's glory, a point already suggested on p. 69. The *Benedicite* expresses this view, and many Christian saints and poets have so understood the natural order.

To see the world as manifestation and celebration imposes a particular attitude to it. We are led to respect and trust nature, to explore it in the confidence that what we find can be part of our apprenticeship of praise. We learn to affirm the diversity and gratuitous abundance of creation in its own right. Like the writer of the Book of Job, we can see God's glory even in the remote and (humanly) irrelevant aspects of the universe. The grand sweep of evolutionary process is part of this vision: out of cosmic history emerged beings capable of praising God through lives of conscious freedom, acknowledged dependence and respectful authority. In humanity the praises of creation find an articulate voice.

Such an understanding provides both a test and an affirmation for the work of science and technology. We ask how well they glorify God through the enlightenment of our imaginations and the enablement of our activity. A similar affirmation and challenge is presented to the artist. The key is the belief that God's fundamental act is the sharing of the divine life, diffused and reflected throughout creation. For human beings that reflection is expressed in the generosity of love, that love demonstrated and set free in the cross and resurrection of Christ.

Our theology must look beyond the narrowly Christian or the narrowly human whilst retaining its Christ-centred vision.

Because the nature of God's intended new humanity is revealed in liberation from self-assertion, a Christian theology of art and nature can furnish a critique of a distorted anthropocentrism. A prophetic word is to be spoken against fantasies of absolute control and unlimited exploitation. Humanity is not empowered to exercise a ruthless domination, cutting down rain forests for short-term gain, but it is called to a careful stewardship, preserving the integrity of the earth's environment. We must seek a technology that is genuinely oriented towards living in and with creation, working with the grain of nature and taking seriously its ecological balance. There can be no absolutizing of immediate human wants, and we must struggle against a technocracy which fails to have a sense of our belonging to this whole planet.

Yet we also acknowledge that we have every scientific reason to suppose that eventually the sun will explode, killing all life on earth and that, even more remotely, the whole universe will collapse or decay. While these predictions lie billions of years in the future, they serve to warn us against any facile utopianism within the course of present physical process. In the end, even the universe's fruitfulness will prove to have been a transient episode. We need not be dismayed, for in the end the only source of lasting hope is God. 'The whole creation has been groaning in travail together until now; and not only the creation, but we ourselves, who have the first fruits of the Spirit, groan inwardly as we wait for adoption as sons, the redemption of our bodies... If we hope for what we do not see, we wait for it with patience' (Rom.8.22ff.). The patient working of the Spirit within physical process will find its final completion in the transcendent act of bringing about a redeemed new creation, beyond present physical process, a point which will be developed in our concluding chapter. However, before we consider the consummation of all things, we devote a chapter to a point on which in this chapter we have touched but briefly, namely artistic and intellectual creativity, and we seek there also to discern the Spirit's work.

9

The Spirit and Creativity

The subject of our last chapter, divine creation, would seem to
lead naturally into reflection on the theme of human creativity. Indeed, that very opening chapter of the Bible which tells
us of the divine creation also speaks of our being in the divine
image (Gen. 1.26f.); thus some sort of analogy between divine
making and human making, however remote, must be implied, and it goes without saying that the divine making is
qualitatively unique. Both in creation and salvation it has the
power to make the wholly new, what in the language of later
theology came to be described as *creatio ex nihilo.* Though in
the Old Testament this may be only implicit, none the less the
qualitative difference is just as much stressed through the use
of a different word for divine, as distinct from human creativity (the Hebrew *bara*). Yet even with this qualitative difference fully acknowledged, the analogy remains. Sometimes
this has meant that the term creativity has itself beeen used to
express the character of the relation, but more commonly
some more particular feature of human making has been highlighted. Two of the most common aspects associated with the
divine image in human creativity are the rationality of human
activity and its free character, both of which set us apart from
the animal world. They have also been used to underpin two
very different approaches to the arts. They will therefore form
a recurring but contrasting theme in what follows. First we
must set these two models against a wider biblical background.

The opening chapter of John's gospel has a richness of
meaning which defies easy translation into other thought
forms. Even so the reader who knows only English must at

the very least take away from the passage the astonishing claim that Jesus is the expression (the 'Word') for what God is like. The opening verse with its deliberate parallel to the opening verse of Genesis ('In the beginning...') shows that even more is at stake, something which becomes much more obvious when we realise that the Greek word *Logos* means not just 'word' or 'expression' but 'explanation' or 'intelligibility'. Moreover it is not too hard to understand how the one word may be used to convey what may initially seem to us very different ideas, for any attempt to make something intelligible involves trying to express it in words. However that may be, the point of the comparison is that, just as the divine *fiat,* the divine word, brought intelligibility and order to the earth which 'was without form and void' (Gen. 1.2), so now we know Jesus to be the key to the intelligibility of our own lives and indeed the life of the world as a whole, for 'all things were made through him' (John 1.3).

In John's gospel it is the Spirit who will teach all things (John 14.26) and will bear witness (John 15.26) to the Son who is this Word. So we may legitimately infer that it is the Spirit who makes possible our perceiving of Jesus as the clue to the world's intelligibility. The Old Testament of course makes no such attributions to specific persons of the Trinity. What we do find is the insistence that the discovery of a rational order to the world is a divine gift and that perception of this is equally the gift of God. The whole of what we now call the Wisdom literature stands in testimony to this. To many of us today much of this literature, such as the Book of Proverbs or Ecclesiastes, may seem all too worldly advice, but there is no doubt that for the Bible such perceptivity into the way things are was taken as indicative of closeness to God, as in the magnificent description of Wisdom 'playing' before God in Proverbs 8.30f. or in the lyrical equation of Law and Wisdom in Ecclesiasticus 24. Occasionally also the fact of this 'spirit of wisdom' being a divine gift is highlighted by its being portrayed as conveyed through a rite of laying on of hands (cf. e.g. Deut. 34.9). Thus there is firm biblical precedent for

148

understanding the divine image in us as, among other things, that rational perception of the world's order given to us by participation in the divine Spirit.

On the other hand another very different understanding of the image is also available. It need not be seen as in conflict with the model described above, but as a matter of fact it often has been. It finds its natural point in doubts whether the rationality of the world and God's purposes for it are as readily accessible as the other tradition often seems to maintain. Might it not be the case that human creativity, so far from being a matter of perceiving what is already there for all to see, is really a question of transcending the way a fallen world is, of breaking out, of discovering through God's grace a new order of existence, one to be achieved by us as we live under a new order of freedom, which is very different from the free choices which have embroiled us in the world of sin? From such a picture it is not hard to derive the idea of reason and religion being opposed, and thus also the creativity of the spiritual world being in opposition to the world of reason. That is a shallow view, but it is important to be aware of the way in which the Bible can be used to generate such an account, as it has played an influential role in one of the two approaches to the arts which we shall consider later. In fact it is possible to derive from both Old and New Testaments the view that creativity is essentially a matter of our being caught up by the Spirit into a new order of existence and thus of our sharing in the creative work of God. Thus, while a passage like Exodus 35.30ff. portrays the Spirit as enabling the ordered work of craftsmanship, there are plenty of other passages to suggest that the Spirit operates more like an invasive power which transcends our natural faculties. Think for instance of the way in which Israel's Judges seem suddenly to acquire their powers without any obvious reference to natural leadership (e.g. Judges 3.10; 6.34; 14.6), or the manner in which prophets are portrayed as acting under an ecstatic trance (e.g. 1 Sam. 10.6; 19.23f.). Again in the New Testament it is tempting to read Paul's frequent contrast between the freedom of the Christian in the

Spirit and the slavery of the Law as implying the superiority of the Christian to all rules. One might also recall that probably the best-known verse in the New Testament about the nature of spirit speaks of it blowing 'where it wills' (John 3.8).

A spontaneous freedom and a constrictive rationality are thereby contrasted instead of their both being seen as integral to any approach which attempts to do justice to the richness of the biblical narrative. That any deeper penetration of the biblical perspective requires their integration would seem obvious. Paul's speech on the Areopagus Hill (Acts 17. esp. vv. 23,28) insists that pagan perception has not gone far enough, not that it contained no truth. In his own writings Paul seems prepared to admit that our freedom as Christians is exercised within the context of the endowments which God has given us by nature, and that the Spirit operates through and develops these natural endowments. Elsewhere in the Bible we find this principle at work: for instance, Peter, who had a certain rock-like quality, became through the Spirit a more reliable rock.

We have mentioned these two models for understanding the way in which human making reflects the divine, not primarily so as to discuss the biblical approach in its own right but in order to provide a framework which will enable us to think better and more deeply about an issue of vital importance for our own times, this question of creativity. So concerned have Christians been with the divine paradigm that we have failed to give adequate attention to two major concerns of our own society: first, the crisis about the meaning of human labour, and secondly, the role of the arts in human self-understanding. The biblical world was one in which there was little or no choice about the sort of work one pursued and one in which many of the art forms which are now so prominent in our lives formed no part (e.g. novels, painting, cinema, television). That does not mean that the Bible can have nothing to say to us on the matter, but it does mean that we must think deeply in order to perceive the connection.

In the case of work, the Bible unhesitatingly declares this

good and ordained by God: man is put into the Garden of Eden 'to till it and keep it' (Gen. 2.15). Such stewardship of the divine creation had already inherent within it an intrinsic intelligibility and order. Whether one pursued a nomadic or an agricultural form of life, this stewardship meant maintaining the order that God had already given to nature, either through activities like feeding the flocks and lambing or through attention to the cycle of the seasons and the rotation of the crops. It is this order that we find reflected in the Old Testament feasts (Passover with its unleavened bread marking the beginning of the barley harvest, Pentecost the end of the wheat harvest, and Tabernacles the autumn fruit harvest). All that changed with the Industrial Revolution and with the micro-chip revolution which has succeeded it. Many people are now much more free about the choice of job they pursue, but there has also come with that a crisis of meaning: whether in our making there is after all any intelligibility to be discovered in what we do (apart from the obvious fact of the necessity of making money to earn our keep). Through the centuries much toil has been experienced as tedious, not merely because the work is routine, but precisely because the worker fails to perceive himself as a true part of the process that gives order and intelligibility to what he is making; the final product appears to bear no intrinsic relationship to his own role. More recently the same problem has expressed itself in new ways. Think how once skilled jobs like an engine driver or print worker have with the new technology become quickly learnt, and how this has led to a crisis of meaning for the worker who continues to pursue the same occupation. He has ceased to be a maker, an imposer of intelligibility on his world; instead he has become a mere operator, someone who sets the process in motion but who cannot really take the credit for the way it turns out.

Thus it would seem that for many of us the modern world of work is pulling in two opposed directions so far as the divine image is concerned. On the one hand, there is far more freedom about what we do than there ever has been in the history of the world, but, on the other, with this has gone a decline in the need for the exercise of our own imposition of intelligibility upon the world. The machine is already there, providing it. This is an issue which industrial psychologists take with increasing seriousness, but reflection upon it within Christianity, unfortunately, still remains in its infancy. Yet, if this imposition of order is an essential part of what it is to be truly human and of what it is to be in the divine image, then we have clear justification for Christian involvement in issues of the workplace: for instance in ways whereby work can be given greater meaning by worker participation in the process as a whole, or in the refusal to reduce human labour to a role purely subordinate to that of the machine. Such reflections remind us that the problem of unemployment is much deeper than the loss of earnings, devastating though that always is. The loss of one's job is also the loss of a chance to impose meaning on the way the world is, and thus to gain recognition from others that one's contribution is worthwhile.

The sharp distinction between artisan and artist with which we are all so familiar dates back only to the fifteenth century. As a symbol of changing attitudes one may note that it is only with the Renaissance that the framing of pictures began; their framing deliberately set them apart. It is also at this time that one begins to get the stress on development and originality that was to become such a marked feature of the Romantic Movement in the late eighteenth and early nineteenth century. This stress is a marked feature of Vasari's *Lives of the Artists* which was published in 1550.

Intellectual history is seldom simple, but as a rough characterization we may say that at the Renaissance one understanding of the arts began to give place to another, though the victory for the latter was decisively won only with the Romantic Movement. For simplicity's sake we may therefore call the earlier view the classical view of the arts, and the later the romantic, though the reader should recall that both these terms have often been used in a variety of other ways. That change of perception can also be said to correspond to a change from one model to another among the two ways of understanding the divine image which we outlined above. The earlier, classical conception of the artist saw him helping us to identify more closely the order already inherent in the divine creation, and indeed he also saw himself doing this within the context of an existing tradition. By contrast the Renaissance began to stress the free role of the individual, a view further accentuated by the Romantic Movement. The free, innovative, unpredictable character of art then became the norm, and the concern was not with the discernment of a rational order in things but with the evocation of feeling and one's response to it.

Temperamentally people are often much more attracted to one form of artistic expression than another. In music, for instance, for some Bach and Mozart are taken as the norm, while for others music only really begins with Beethoven's Third Symphony and the Romantic composition to which that gave birth. But we must be on our guard against making our theories correspond to our prejudices. The later Romantic understanding of the artist was motivated just as much by religious concerns as was the earlier model. It is perhaps initially easier to understand why a concern with order should be seen in essentially religious terms and so why Barth could write of Mozart that 'hearing creation unresentfully and impartially, he did not produce merely his own music but that of creation'. Equally we find that great theorist of the Romantic Movement, Samuel Taylor Coleridge, declaring the imagination to be 'a repetition in the finite mind of the eternal act of creation'. What had happened is that religion (and indeed society in general) had lost its trust in the power of human beings to break through to a perception of the rational, and so, if another world was to be known at all, it had to be known through another medium, through the response of the imagination and emotions to the inspired prophet. The change of attitude is well illustrated by Goya's etching in the Prado in Madrid, *The Dream of Reason Produces Monsters,* or, if a more religious painter is preferred, we recall William Blake's portrayal of Newton with his eyes firmly fixed on the ground and his comment that 'he who sees the Ratio sees only himself'. Inevitably in such a major cultural movement it would be misleading to suggest that only one position was adopted towards reason. Probably more common than Goya's stress on the distorting power of reason would have been the suggestion that the power of reason is strictly limited and should take second place to such notions as insight, feeling, imagination and intuition. Perhaps the difference is best illustrated by William Blake's portrayal of the Trinity (Plate 3). In it a massive, hovering bird, the inspiring Spirit, is given central place, and the crucified Christ is seen with body curved and arms outstretched being drawn by the Father in imaginative flight towards that same Spirit. Readers will no doubt already have spotted some parallel between, on the one hand, the romantic and the classical and, on the other, the work of the Holy Spirit, for it is possible to discern the work of the Spirit in bringing both invention and order. Yet, just as in the explicitly religious case it is difficult to determine the proper balance between free innovation and ordered rationality, so is the problem, if anything, more acute in the artistic case. Here all we can do is to provide a few pointers to enable readers to reflect more deeply on the issue for themselves. We shall take each of the two major approaches in turn, and note a few of the points, both positive and negative, which can be made in respect of each.

To describe, as in the classical model, the artist's role as one of enabling us to see the order and intelligibility in the world, may seem to make the artist redundant. Can we not already perceive it easily enough for ourselves? But the fact that we have eyes to see does not mean that we use them to see. The artist can thus help us to perceive what might otherwise pass us by unnoticed. Think for instance of symbolic connections made in medieval stained glass between the various decisive events in the biblical story, or the links made between the life, death and resurrection of the incarnate Lord and the people and events of the artists' own day. Stanley Spencer's portrayal of the involvement in the crucifixion of his fellow villagers in Cookham in Berkshire ensures that we cannot artificially divorce Pilate, Caiaphas and the crowd from the England of our own day.

Nor should we suppose that such perceptivity is confined to explicitly religious art. Indeed art critics have often drawn attention to the way in which what appears to be a purely secular subject can have a profoundly religious character. This would seem particularly so of the landscape painting of sixteenth- and seventeenth-century Holland. It is not that the artists were retreating into secular themes, in what remained after all still a deeply religious nation. Rather, it is that the Calvinist ethos now perceived God within the perfect balance of landscape; there was no need to point to another world in order to establish symmetry and balance, especially as in any case this would have involved the dangerous use of 'images'. Again, the scientist's work is not explicitly religious, but it remains true that many practising scientists have experienced something bordering upon religious awe and wonder at the nature of the order in the universe which they have made known to us. This certainly includes the most famous physicist of our century, Albert Einstein whose attitude was one of wonder and submission to the way things are. Indeed one of his most famous remarks ('God does not play dice') was a response to Heisenberg's uncertainty principle, and indicates his reluctance to allow that there could be an element of unpredictability and so an element of 'disorder' in the universe. Likewise theoretical physicists like Paul Dirac have used the search for mathematical beauty as a powerful guiding principle in their research. Towards the end of this chapter we shall suggest ways in which the creative work of the scientist may be understood in terms of the activity of the Holy Spirit.

Yet at the same time we should be on our guard against supposing that perception of structure and order necessarily leads to a religious response. Indeed even in the case of great painting the structure and religion may be fundamentally opposed. The Cubism of Picasso's *Les Demoiselles d'Avignon*

155

may well be a case in point. Does not Picasso in this painting reduce the unfortunate prostitutes of Avignon Street in Barcelona to mere impersonal structures, mere things? Yet at other times even when there is no explicit connection with our faith, the Christian cannot but be grateful to the artist for opening his eyes to the way things are. Solzhenitsyn made the point thus in his Nobel Prize speech: 'Art and literature can perform the miracle of overcoming man's characteristic weakness of learning only by his own experience, so that the experience of others passes him by... Art recreates in the flesh all experience lived by other men, so that each man can make this his own.' Almost all of us have had that experience in reading a novel and seeing the plight of others in a new light for the first time; we feel ourselves chastened for lack of insight into ourselves and for lack of compassion towards others.

In an influential book on Christian aesthetics the French philosopher Jacques Maritain defined beauty as 'intellect delighting in matter intelligibly arranged'. This well reflects this particular tradition in art. Aquinas for instance insisted upon three criteria for beauty: proportion, integrity and clarity. By proportion he meant essentially order or balance: by integrity fitting shape or size (small people on his view cannot be beautiful); and by clarity luminosity, the right balance of colour and light so that an object stands out appropriately. His view and that of his contemporaries that there is a right measure for everything may well seem to most of us today as absurdly over-confident. Indeed there is a whole genre of theological reasoning based on such criteria that has now vanished and which seems strangely foreign to us. How often for instance will one ever hear a sermon today on the way in which the Cross as the tree of life was deliberately intended by God as a balance to the tree that brought death in the Garden of Eden? Even the circle no longer carries the same immediate symbolic resonances as it would once have done. For those firmly entrenched in the classical tradition it was the most beautiful of geometrical figures because the most perfectly proportioned (the circumference always equidistant from the centre), and it is for this reason that it was deemed legitimate to use the symbolism even of God. In Rublev's icon of the Trinity (Plate 4) it is somewhat hidden, but one does find on inspection that the external outline of the three angels employed to represent the Trinity when joined together do constitute a perfect circle. The intention is to indicate not just perfection, but also indissolubility, since the circle, unlike lined figures, has no obvious parts. However, perhaps a better example than the Rublev icon, and certainly one more pertinent to our theme of the Spirit, is a mosaic from the Baptistery in Albenga in northern Italy (Plate 6), dating from the fifth century. Here the Holy Spirit is represented as a perfect circle of doves encompassing Christ's monogram. In other words, in striking contrast to the Blake drawing to which we referred earlier (Plate 3), the Holy Spirit, so far from being seen as the key to imaginative flight, is viewed as the source of access to perfect order and proportion.

Another feature of this tradition which has all but vanished from our thinking is the ascription to God of beauty itself, not just in the weak sense that God is its source but in the strong sense that God's very being is beautiful. We are still prepared today to speak of God being Goodness itself or Truth itself, but what we need to recall is that for our ancestors in the faith it was once just as natural to speak of God's being Beauty itself. So for example in a famous passage in his *Confessions* Augustine does not hesitate to write of God: 'Late have I loved thee, O Beauty'. The use of such language exudes confidence in a wholly integrated world. The creation as perfect balance and proportion is for all its beauty but a pale reflection of the creator, who is perfect beauty. One reason, perhaps the principal reason, for this attribution was the conviction that what made a proportion beautiful was its intrinsic simplicity, and that therefore simplicity itself must be beautiful. But, if that is so, the argument goes, then God is the most beautiful of all beings because God is the most simple, in the sense that one has only to think of one of the divine attributes and immediately the others are seen to be implied. For instance, it was commonly argued that one who knows all thereby also knows the good and thus is goodness itself. Also, one who is truly good would be inhibited from the perfect exercise of goodness unless possessing complete power to bring this goodness to fruition.

Today we no longer share the same confidence in such arguments. It is, however, worth drawing attention to the way in which one major theologian of the twentieth century has attempted to revive this tradition for us, but in a way which takes seriously the fact that we live in a post-romantic world, namely, Hans Urs von Balthasar (d.1988), whose major work *The Glory of the Lord: A Theological Aesthetics* is currently being translated into English. Though a Roman Catholic, he has been heavily influenced by two major Protestant theologians, Kierkegaard and Barth; and this is reflected in the way in which he looks through the lens of revelation at the numerous writers whom he examines and evaluates. In effect revelation has become his measuring rod; it is this which secures beyond doubt that his work is no mere attempt simply to return to the past, but rather a serious engagement of the classical tradition with the romantic challenge. Perhaps the difference between von Balthasar's approach and earlier classical accounts could be described by saying that whereas the latter took account of the presence of the creative Word in all things, he refers everything more explicitly to the Word made flesh. In effect what has happened is that notions like *kenōsis* and crucifixion now play a central role, whereas for the earlier classical tradition these were incidental or secondary to a stress on the intelligibility and rationality of creation, as implied in the notion of *Logos*. Of course all Christians would be agreed that the crucified Lord is indispensable to a total understanding of reality; where they differ is whether this means that no part of reality is intelligible without such reference. Perhaps the difference can best be brought out by contrasting the recurring reference to the crucifixion in von Balthasar with the irrepressible optimism, despite his own ill-health, of the poet Alexander Pope. For instance in his *Essay on Man* of 1734 we find him writing:

> All nature is but art unknown to thee;
> All chance, direction which thou canst not see;
> All discord, harmony not understood
> All partial evil, universal good.

There we have the earlier classical tradition's ineradicable confidence in the uncomplicated goodness of the world. By contrast, for someone later in the classical tradition, like von Balthasar, the beauty of an integrated world is hard won, and then only thanks to the gift of revelation. A twentieth-century poet in the classical tradition like T. S. Eliot takes a similar view: 'The life of the soul does not consist in the contemplation of one consistent world, but in the painful task of unifying ... joining incompatible ones, and passing when possible, from two or more discordant viewpoints to a higher which shall somehow include and transmute them'. Some artists have indeed seen and experienced a kind of crucifixion in their creativity; in God's creative activity there is, as it were, simultaneity of cost and joy.

Though von Balthasar and Eliot insist on the pain and difficulty in producing an integrated vision, they remain within the classical tradition because they think it possible. By contrast, it is because of the romantic tradition's lack of confidence in the power of reason that even its religious exponents remain doubtful whether such a reconciliation can become accessible to us. Instead, the role of the artist becomes a much more limited one, namely to evoke within us an imaginative response to the possibility of different worlds and different realities. The difference may perhaps be seen at its starkest in the approach to evil. Whereas for the classical tradition evil has always been to some degree an embarrassment, because it represents something resistant to proportion and elegance, for romantic writers it is often the harshness of reality (including suffering and moral evil), which is seen as the primary vehicle through which God acts; thus part of the artist's role has become to help us to see God through the apparent darkness, in which there is no tidy balance and proportion. So for instance in Evelyn Waugh's *Brideshead Revisited* the narrator Charles Ryder is made to come to faith despite all the odds, and, in so far as it is a response to other human beings in the story, it seems to be precisely because his friend Sebastian remains loyal to his faith despite the fact of its preventing him from being a 'happy and healthy man'; likewise his mistress, Sebastian's sister Julia, leaves him so that she may fulfil a commitment which seems to bear no relation to human happiness. Again, in the novels of Graham Greene it is by plunging his characters into impossible dilemmas and a morass of human suffering that he evokes from them the response of faith. As a yet more extreme example one might consider the case of Flannery O'Connor, a Catholic novelist from Georgia in the United States. Were readers unaware of her own personal suffering and the very moving character of her letters, we might well be forgiven for thinking that the intention of her stories was simply to create some awful piece of black humour rather than to open our eyes to the terrible consequence of our own prejudices and to the redemptive character of suffering. Again, if one turns to the world of painting, Georges Rouault is one of the great Christian painters of the century, but his attitude to the world's ugliness is romantic, not classical. It is only by bringing us face to face with all the nastiness of life that he believes it is possible to evoke from us the response of faith; hence his series of etchings called *Miserere* and his pictures of prostitutes.

The issues are too complex to be resolved quickly here. Readers must be left to themselves to decide whether the response of feeling to the world's agonies better represents a Christian approach to art as the romantic might well say, or whether the classical emphasis on the divine goodness inherent in the world is more accurate. It would be good if we could solve the dilemma by simply saying that we need both. That is already to compromise and weaken both positions. So probably in the end we must decide that one or other more accurately reflects the way in which God has placed us in the world.

The Spirit and Creativity

Fortunately with another of the romantic challenges to the classical position, the claim that we are more than a mere reasoning faculty, it is much easier to weigh the rights and wrongs of the argument. We shall look first at the ways in which the romantic insistence on feeling and imagination can be seen justly to earn their place; then we shall consider how the argument can be carried too far in valuing any and every sort of expressiveness for its own sake.

The Church can justly be proud of its patronage of the arts both in the past and to some extent still today. But it is as well to recall that such recognition has often been hard won, and that this resistance was more often than not due to the suspicion that feeling and imagination could only detract from, rather than enhance, a true faith. Part of the worry was no doubt the Old Testament's prohibition of images, and the conviction expressed by it that the nature of God is beyond all human attempts either to conceptualize or even to imagine. Another concern was almost certainly associated with the truth that God is unembodied; access to God must, therefore, be through that part of our being which most resembles God, namely our reasoning faculties, rather than through the emotions which seem essentially bound up with our nature as physical beings. Both worries are fundamentally misconceived. Nowadays some Christians assume that such worries about the distorting and distracting power of art were products of the Reformation, but in fact they long antedate the sixteenth century. One need only recall the iconoclastic controversy of the eighth century and Emperor Leo III's attempts to prohibit all icons, or the attacks of Bernard of Clairvaux in the twelfth century on the distracting intricacies of Romanesque art, or Aquinas' reluctance in the thirteenth to have any other than unaccompanied singing in church. Nevertheless, while we take seriously the possibility of distortion, our basic attitude on this matter can never be that of the Old Testament, for the simple reason that God who is beyond our imagining has taken a concrete icon or image in the person of Jesus Christ. So it is hard to see how one could condemn artis-

161

tic representation without condemning the divine artist's self-portrayal. Artists take up pen or brush, and in doing so they do something analogous to God's activity (in which the Spirit had a full share) both in creation and in the incarnation; indeed all Christians can do something similar when through the Spirit they seek to model their lives after the pattern of Christ. As for the other worry of distraction, there are two ways in which art might distract from bringing us into closer relation with God, and both seem mistaken worries, though for rather different reasons. First, it might draw us away from the exercise of our reason. That is true, but why should this always be viewed negatively? We are more than disembodied spirits, and this is presumably taken into account in the range of ways in which God chooses to communicate with us. Secondly, if the point rather is that the seductive power of art is such that it makes us contemplate the work itself as distinct from using it purely as a vehicle towards God, this is a false contrast, for it is precisely because we value things in and for themselves that we are often led on to God. It is because we value other human beings in their own right that we are led to see them as an image of God; precisely because we value truth for itself, we come to see in God the source of all truth, and so on; in short, precisely because we value other things unconditionally, we come to see meaning in God as pre-eminently the unconditioned.

The artist David Jones in an influential essay has spoken of the 'gratuitous' character of all art. In so doing he intended to draw a contrast with a purely utilitarian approach, and he insists that even in ordinary human work this is what raises it above the merely animal, that here is a free expressiveness over and above any further ends. Another way of putting this might be to say that, though unlike the divine creation it does not proceed 'from nothing', art properly speaking is none the less 'for nothing'. Inherent in human creative activity is a joy which is not necessarily utilitarian. Eliot indeed refers to the sense of joy in artistic achievement as exhaustion, appeasement, absolution. Further, it needs to be said that we should value such expressiveness simply for its own sake, especially as much of it can be bought at great personal cost. There is something deeply sacrificial in artistic creation, an element of self-negation, not unlike God's own creative work, itself rooted in self-giving. For some artists pain becomes an inescapable element in their struggle to express and give of themselves to others. In such cases it is not unfitting to remark that the artist has come to share something of the life of our Lord himself, he who was the very incarnation of pain and self-giving inextricably intertwined. One instance of the painful cost of creativity may be seen in 'the weeping, walking, breaking his pens, repeating and altering a bar a hundred times' which Georges Sand tells us was composition for Chopin.

Such an approach has its dangers, and such valuing always needs to be set in some wider context. In a world in which gratuitous violence and sex are a routine part of the artistic medium it is salutary to recall the world of little more than a century ago, when a novel as apparently innocuous as *Madame Bovary* was put on trial. What so shocked the Paris of 1857 was merely the portrayal of adultery (not the sexual acts) without accompanying moral comment. There was no attempt to set the presentation in a wider frame of reference, and ever since mere expression has often been taken as sufficient justification of artistic creation. Is this not one case where the classical approach has the edge over the romantic? Though expression definitely has its value (and we are not arguing for censorship), it remains of only limited worth except in so far as it can be integrated into a larger whole. It is for this reason that morality and aesthetics cannot be totally prised apart.

It must, however, be conceded that Christians have frequently taken all too easy a route to such integration. For instance the Cambridge Camden Society which played such a large part in the revival of Gothic architecture in the nineteenth century took the view that only the good and religious man could effectively produce the right kind of architecture

(Decorated Gothic), while only a little later we find the hymn writer, F. W. Faber, declaring in his correspondence that Lord Byron could not have been a great poet because he was not a good man. Life is more complicated than that. Certainly there is no guarantee that great art will necessarily affect the moral quality of people's lives; the officers at Auschwitz saw no incongruity in relaxing to Schubert's music after their dreadful deeds. Equally the equation does not hold the other way round: moral goodness is not a *sine qua non* for great art, (recall, for instance, the scandalous character of Caravaggio's life), nor is it even the case that religious belief is necessary for the production of great religious art. Agnostics like Verdi with his *Requiem* or Mahler with his *Resurrection Symphony,* and not just undoubtedly devout composers like Bruckner, have the power to move us religiously.

Christians remain divided on the question whether the Holy Spirit is active outside the Church as the community of the redeemed, though we have stated our own view on this subject in our introductory chapter (pp. 12f.). Certainly Schleiermacher's readiness to describe a non-Christian philosopher like Spinoza as 'full of the Holy Spirit' would have shocked many a Father of the Church. Even those who wish to say that response to the Spirit is confined within the Church must agree that the Spirit can and does use the work of non-Christians to deepen the response of faith in those who already believe. In other words the Spirit may work through unbelief in much the same way as Second Isaiah once saw God acting through the pagan monarch Cyrus (Is. 45.1), though it would be wrong to say that there was any direct response from Cyrus himself (v.4). The obvious objection to this account remains, that it suggests too manipulative a view of the Spirit's operation in the world. Yet, even if we say that the Spirit always operates in terms of personal response even among non-believers, it will still need to be conceded that the production of artistic genius is often heavily dependent on non-personal factors. Arguably Rembrandt is the greatest religious painter of all time. Yet he learned his use of light and dark contrasts from Caravaggio. Had the latter's style not been condemned by the Roman Catholic Church of the time, the Protestant Rembrandt would probably not have been able to adopt an approach to painting first advocated by this violent and licentious Catholic.

While Christians can thus rightly be criticized in their turn for too often taking too easy a route towards an integrated vision, their criticism of unqualified romantic exaltations of expression for its own sake remains justified. The excessive cult of newness and novelty which seems so often to mar some later developments of this romantic approach may also be justly criticized. We can acknowledge the fact that this romantic cult may well have helped generate the explosion of art forms which the twentieth century has witnessed. Public reaction to these has often been hostile, but Christians too have reason to be grateful for some of the possibilities that have now been realised. For instance Kandinsky and Chagall explored new possibilities for conveying 'the spiritual' by means of colour, Kandinsky even writing a book entitled 'Concerning the Spiritual in Art'; indeed they both did not hesitate to see their art in essentially religious terms. Chagall for instance has commented that, 'Art, painting is religious by nature – like everything creative'. If an explicitly Christian example is preferred, one might think of the way in which one of the great composers of our century, Olivier Messiaen, has pioneered the use of bird song as a way of conveying the presence of the divine to his fellow-believers. Nevertheless we must resist the conclusion that great art has to be innovative to be truly creative. Even the completely unoriginal can be great art. So for example when one steps into one of our great medieval cathedrals, one wonders at its grandeur and beauty, even if every feature of the building finds an exact parallel elsewhere.

The literary critic Helen Gardner has suggested that it is enough if the artist 'makes more vivid to us what we already know and feel'. No doubt this is often so. To make this the norm would however, be to err just as much in the opposite direction. Though the romantic errs who claims that art must offer something wholly new, there nonetheless remains a sense in which most art is after all striving after something new – not new in the sense of totally new to the world, but new in the sense of new perceptions for the artist or for his audience. In the ability of the artist through his work to bring new perceptions to other people, we may see some parallel with the work of the Holy Spirit; they both have a relational element. It is the Holy Spirit who establishes and perfects our relationship with Christ; it is often thanks to art or literature that we are enabled to relate to the world around us in a new way. But, just as the Holy Spirit brings what is only to us wholly new (that same relationship is already a reality for others), so can much the same be said of the role of the artistic medium. It is also often this more limited sense of newness of which artists themselves are speaking, as Aaron Copland has remarked of his composition, 'Each added work brings with it an element of self-discovery ... a part answer to the question "Who am I?"'. We may also use it to explain how our own mundane work or hobbies can be experienced as creatively new. There are of course hundreds of others who have solved exactly the same sort of management problem or created exactly the same sort of herbaceous border, but it is the first time for us, and that is what makes it feel so creatively exciting and rewarding. The same principle applies not only to problem solving in business and to creativity in gardening: it is capable of wide application, for example to the solving of problems in personal relations and to inventiveness and creativity exhibited, say, by a child making clay models or by a student writing an essay.

Such examples, like our earlier discussion of work, remind us that human creativity is much wider than the arts, important though these are. That is why it would be wrong to conclude this discussion without a brief consideration of the natural sciences within the sphere of human creativity. It is one of the great and dangerous myths of our time that there are two cultures, one nurtured by the creative arts, the other by objective science. This false dichotomy, manifested in the division between the so-called Arts and Sciences in education, has been nurtured, among other things, by a powerful but fallacious philosophy of science – that of positivism. Accordingly science is perceived to be a purely empirical enterprise based on the twin pillars of observation and inductive verification. There is little or no room in this scheme for the creative, imaginative, conjectural faculties and consequently science is reckoned to be a cold, dispassionate, objective enterprise in which the human imagination and emotions have no part. Although this philosophy of science has long been discredited it still exercises a grip on the minds of many, including those working scientists and theologians who adopt it unquestioningly. It accounts for a great deal of the disillusionment with science and rationality which is so widespread in our age.

Sir Karl Popper, above all, has devoted his life's work to combating this fallacy and to developing an alternative interpretation which embraces the whole range of human endeavour – the arts, the sciences, and the political institutions within which they function. Bryan Magee in his book on Popper succinctly comments:

> If Popper is right, there are not two cultures – one scientific and the other aesthetic ... but one. The scientist and the artist, far from being engaged in opposed or incompatible activities, are both trying to extend our understanding of experience by the use of creative imagination subjected to critical control.

A passing knowledge of the history of ideas reveals the great scientist not as an impersonal, detached, systematic observer of the world, but rather as a passionate enquirer, displaying the whole range of human faculties and emotions. One can cite the heartrending struggles in the move from the Ptolemaic to the Copernican Solar System; the epoch-making conjecture of Darwin regarding Natural Selection; Einstein's profound imaginative grasp of the structure of space and time that led to the formulation of his relativity theories; the challenging development of quantum theory in the early decades of this century; the fascinating story of the unravelling of the

DNA molecule in the early fifties; and most recently the daring theories of contemporary cosmologists stretching the mind's power of abstract thought to the limit.

This reminds us of a further parallel between the arts and the sciences with regard to problem-solving and the importance of history and tradition. Although we have referred to divine creativity as making wholly new, human creativity must work with existing material. We can never make an entirely new start, either in the arts or in the sciences. That distinguished historian and philosopher of art, Sir Ernst Gombrich, in his book *Art and Illusion* accounts for creativity in the visual arts as Popper accounts for it in the sciences, in terms of the gradual modification of a tradition under the pressure of novel demands. The history of art, like the history of science, is more like a running argument than a series of cataclysmic upheavals.

The creative, imaginative probings of the scientist help to provide a unifying picture of the world and of our part in it. He shares this vision with the religious enquirer for whom the picture cannot be complete unless it is set within the context of divine creativity which is manifested to us as the work of the Holy Spirit of God.

Though such a role for imagination as well as reason in scientific creativity is now very widely acknowledged, it would be misleading to end this chapter on that note of happy balance. Whereas in the sciences the relationship between the two is clear, with imagination providing clues and reason arbitrating, there is no such easy truce in the arts between the classical and romantic traditions. That is why in the course of this chapter we have felt it necessary to leave some issues between them unresolved. However, let us end on a positive note about both. The romantic tradition must be right in insisting that our response to God is about our whole being responding and not just our reason; thus the emotions and the imagination too must play their part, as equally the creation of God. On the other hand, in taking this into account we must not lose sight of the classical tradition's insistence on an integrated vision. Even if the romantic is right that most of it must remain hidden in this life, it still remains true that ultimately this is where the Spirit is calling us. It is to that integrated vision of a new order, the final destiny to which all the world is called, to the vision of our future in the Spirit that we next turn.

10

The Holy Spirit and the Future

Every chapter of this book implies a decisive connection between the Holy Spirit and the future. We have spoken of the experience of the Holy Spirit. This present experience comes as an anticipation of what is destined to be enjoyed more fully in the future. We have spoken of the Spirit and Christ. Experience of the Spirit is bound up with our being in Christ because we share in advance his resurrection life and resurrection mode of existence, even if this is hidden before the general resurrection of the dead (Col.3. 1ff.). The power of the Spirit, of which we have also spoken, represents an anticipation of the future, releasing us from bondage to the past. Nevertheless, as we have seen, this power is shaped by the pattern of the cross. For the present it remains power-in-weakness, for Pentecost lies on the yonder side of Calvary, but also comes as a gift reserved for the 'last days' (Acts 2. 16 ff.).

Other chapters have introduced further themes which belong to the future. The Church is the community of the Holy Spirit, the members of which will share in the final victory when all shall be well. But meanwhile the Church yearns for a freedom and fulfilment which is only in process of being brought about. The present work of the Spirit in the Church represents the first fruits of what is to come: 'We ourselves, who have the first fruits of the Spirit, groan inwardly as we wait for adoption as sons, the redemption of our bodies' (Rom.8.23). The sacraments offer pledges of God's covenant faithfulness to his promises 'until he comes' (1 Cor.11.26), and all is publicly fulfilled. Truth is disclosed through the Spirit definitively in Christ; but our grasp of this truth remains partial and imperfect until everything can be seen in the light of the whole. We shall see more clearly the truth of the world and of history, in a sense, only when the whole is complete. But in advance of this context every judgement remains open to revision in the light of such truth. The truth of the Holy Spirit is therefore closely connected with the notion of a definitive revelation of the whole, traditionally represented through language about the Last Judgement. The Paraclete in the fourth gospel is the one who comes alongside to help and defend; but the Spirit also places men and women at the bar of such judgement in advance of its occurrences. The Spirit 'convicts' or 'exposes' to the human heart what will be publicly and openly demonstrable only at the last day (John 14.16ff; 16. 7ff.).

Our discussions of the Spirit and the world, and of creativity, pointed to the reality of the Holy Spirit as the one beyond and yet within. The Spirit comes as God in transcendence and as God in God's immanence. In early Christian faith it seemed natural to use spatial imagery to express this 'beyond': God and divine activity were conceived as being 'above' the world. The divine Spirit transcended the realm of human comprehension, whether of conceptual thought or imagination. But biblical formulations did not rely exclusively on spatial imagery to express this transcendence or beyondness. For the writer to the Hebrews, faith is 'the assurance of things hoped for' (Heb.11.1.). Faith is directed towards the invisible not only in the sense of that which lies beyond the material world, but also in the sense of its being directed towards God's promises and power to bring about that which is unseen because it has not yet become reality. In this sense, the Holy Spirit brings forward a reality which is grounded in divine promise rather than in human thought or achievement. Even though in processes of creativity the Spirit of God works through the instrumentality of natural processes and through the agency of human thought and imagination, we can never reduce the reality of the Spirit in such a way as to equate it with these processes exhaustively and without remainder.

Without some reference to 'the last things' of Christian

faith it is difficult to determine what movements are to count as constructive from some intermediate vantage point in history. The old debates between those who saw creative meaning in terms of supernatural purpose and those who saw it in terms of natural or emergent processes cannot be settled simply by invoking some principle of immanent purposive process, such as we find in classical forms of Marxism. As we saw in the chapter on creation, modern scientific theories explore the interplay of order and disorder, of structure and flux, in ways which help us to discard an outmoded picture of a closed universe predetermined by a tight chain of cause and effect. They help us to see how novelty and creativity can emerge without recourse to hypotheses about interruptions of natural processes. Nevertheless, these do not take us beyond an account of the processes themselves. They offer models which facilitate our understanding of the creative processes through which the Spirit operates, but they do not plumb the depths of the ultimate reality which is the ground of their possibility and the End which gives them definitive meaning.

How the new and innovative is related to the future is seen more clearly in the realm of redemption. In the New Testament the experience of the Holy Spirit is an experience of release and freedom. In Paul, this stands in contrast to bondage to the law. But law, in this context, means more than obligation to obey divine commandments, for these laws continue to have relevance within the new creation, and the Spirit calls us to the obedience of sonship. Neither is bondage to the law simply a matter of pressure to conform with the particular traditions of Judaism. The issue is wider than this. Human beings remain under the law as long as the determining principles of their lives emerge out of their own past decisions and actions, and out of past choices and values reflected in human cultures and societies. Men and women are bound by the limited range of options which emerge from their own past. Theologically, the most serious of these is the circle of negative processes set up by being caught in a net of sin, guilt, weakness, and the law.

Into this network of bondage enters the liberating power of the Holy Spirit. In place of guilt and estrangement, we read of 'the Spirit ... bearing witness with our spirit that we are children of God' (Rom. 8.16), that 'the Spirit helps us in our weakness' (Rom. 8.26), and that 'the law (i.e. cause-effect processes) of the Spirit of life in Christ Jesus has set me free from the law of sin and death' (Rom. 8.2). All this is seen in the New Testament as a breaking in of the future. I am determined by the future God has promised rather than by the past I have made. The gift of the Holy Spirit in the present is only the beginning of the harvest proper, of which it is a foretaste (Rom. 8.23). This experience of the Spirit is that of sonship, whereby we share Jesus' intimacy with God as 'Abba', 'dear Father' (Rom. 8.14ff.). This is described as a right to inheritance: to be a son is to be an heir (Rom. 8.17). Christians will receive what Christ has received, and they look forward to a future glory (Rom. 8.18). They 'wait with eager longing' for the redemption of the body; for God to fulfil in their whole person what God has promised (Rom. 8.19ff.).

Sonship, redemption, and freedom all have future aspects, yet to be fulfilled. But because the Spirit has already been given as the first-fruits of a harvest to come, the future is guaranteed. The future is anticipated, as it were, in advance. The Spirit is the 'earnest of the inheritance' or 'guarantee' of this future (2 Cor.1.22; 5.5). What is guaranteed is the fulfilment of God's promises, the inheritance of redemption, and a resurrection mode of existence characterised by the Spirit. In the power of the Holy Spirit human persons can begin to be what they are to become. The first three gospels use language about the kingdom of God which is also both present and future. There is a parallel between our standing between the kingdom inaugurated and the kingdom accomplished and our standing between the gift of the Spirit as first-fruits and the Spirit's coming in fullness.

On several occasions in the course of this study we have touched on the work of the Holy Spirit in connection with healing (e.g. in Chapters 3 and 6). It is appropriate in this chapter entitled 'The Holy Spirit and the Future' to refer once again to the work of the Holy Spirit in this connection. We have noted the elements both present and future in the sonship, redemption and freedom brought by the Spirit; in these respects Christian people have been given through the Spirit a real, though partial, anticipation of that which they may confidently expect to be fulfilled hereafter. We have also observed how this is congruent with the material in Jesus' teaching contained in the first three gospels, in which the kingdom of God is understood to be both present and future. In this material there are links between the Spirit, the kingdom of God and healing, for instance in the version of Jesus' saying to be found in Matthew's gospel, in connection with his exorcism of a blind and dumb man (Matt.12.28). In the version of Jesus' sermon in the synagogue at Nazareth in Luke's gospel (Lk.4.16ff.) we find the Spirit particularly associated with his work of healing; in this passage the idea of the kingdom of God is not far distant. Readers of the Acts of the Apostles are given to understand that the Spirit who rested upon Jesus is now active in the Christian Church and thus that the healings done by Peter and Paul are done through the Spirit present and active in the Church.

We need to apply the same principle with regard to healing, as with sonship, redemption and freedom. The healing done through the Spirit by Jesus, by the apostles in the early Church, and subsequently in Christ's name within the Church's history is real and effective, though of necessity only partial and temporary in the present life. Already the firstfruits of the Spirit are a real, true and present possession given to Christian people; through these first-fruits we are given future hope and grounds of confident expectation that fulfilment, understood in this context in terms of healing complete and enduring, will be given us through the Spirit hereafter. This healing may be outward, physical and visible; certainly it will be secret and hidden, deep in the centre of the human person. This latter activity is generally beyond the conscious awareness of people, for the Spirit touches and teaches the heart. Thus the Spirit's healing and transforming influence works outwards, gradually correcting humans' thinking, feeling and spontaneous reactions, gradually bringing forth the fruit of the Spirit, which will be harvested in its fullness hereafter.

Meanwhile, however, the present experience of the Holy Spirit cannot be isolated from the ambiguities which characterize the present. Even within the New Testament period the difficulty of trying to offer watertight or unambiguous criteria of the Spirit's operation and presence is acknowledged as we have already recognized in Chapter 3. In 1 Corinthians, members of the community make great play of their status as 'spiritual people'. Yet where there is jealousy and strife, Paul cannot address them as people controlled by the Spirit (1 Cor. 3. 1-3). He redefines true 'spirituality' in the light of the cross, and within a framework of what builds up the whole community in love. Nevertheless, love remains a quality which belongs to the new order of the future. The poem on love which forms the centrepiece of Paul's discussion of spiritual gifts (1 Cor. 12-14) makes it clear that the Corinthian community has not yet reached full maturity in this respect. Many are still boastful, jealous, arrogant, and at times insistent on their own way (cf. 1 Cor. 13.5). Love will relativize the other gifts, because love alone will never become obsolete through changing circumstances and conditions: 'love never ends; as for prophecy, it will pass away; as for tongues, they will cease; as for knowledge, it will pass away' (1 Cor. 13.8). Until it can reflect that quality of love which still lies in the future, the Church's claims to speak with the voice of the Holy Spirit must remain qualified by a persistent ambiguity, which invites careful discernment.

In the period from the New Testament to modern times, the history of the Christian Church underlines the fact of this ambiguity. No movement of the Church's life, whether of spiritual revival, or of spiritual renewal, or of its institutional developments, has ever been free from ambiguities which reflect human failures or exaggerations alongside the work of the Spirit. Neither the voice of the Church nor that of its critics can be identified absolutely and unambiguously with the voice of the Spirit before the consummation of its deliverance from weakness and sin. Paul Tillich insisted that this was an implication of what he called 'the Protestant principle'. He writes: 'The paradox of the churches is the fact that they participate, on the one hand, in the ambiguities of life in general and of the religious life in particular, and on the other hand, in the unambiguous life of the Spiritual Community' (*Systematic Theology* vol. 3, p. 176). This has been expressed, he adds, in the traditional distinction between the Church invisible and visible. The Church is holy, one, and universal, in as far as the Holy Spirit has in principle made the Church what God destines it to become in the Spirit's grace and power. But the Creator-Spirit's work is not yet complete. There may even be fallibility and self-interest, manipulation and desire for power where there are movements in the Church which may otherwise represent movements of the Holy Spirit. Only when the future destiny of the Church becomes manifest, and the work of the Spirit is complete within it, will this ambiguity dissolve, to give place to an unmixed manifestation of the Spirit's creative and renewing work.

This should make us hesitate to judge the nature of the future in the light of the present, or to equate what we see of the Spirit's work now with that which is yet to be. No responsible critic will judge an artist's work while it is still in the making. 'Do not pronounce judgement before the time' (1 Cor. 4.5). To change the metaphor into those of the Matthean parables, only at harvest time can the weeds be finally separated from the wheat, or only in the boat or on the shore can the good fish be separated from the bad ones (Matt. 13. 24ff.; 47ff.). 'Now I know in part; then I shall understand fully' (1 Cor. 13.12). Even given an awareness of what it is to experience the Holy Spirit, it is still possible, ahead of future growth and maturity, to speak, to think, and to reason 'like a child'. The indirect and sometimes enigmatic reflections perceived in a bronze mirror are not to be confused with the reality which we wait to see face to face (1 Cor. 13.12).

At the same time, we should not make the opposite mistake. Because the Holy Spirit determines this future, it is not entirely adequate to say that such a future is in principle *totally* beyond all potential human experience or completely beyond the range of crude or provisional human understanding. For the Holy Spirit, as the first-fruits of our inheritance, also represents a foretaste of a reality of which more is to come. The yearnings and longings, as well as the joys and promises, which the Spirit of God places in the human heart do not stand in sharp discontinuity with the promised future. Newness of life stands both in contrast to, and in continuity with, the old. For Christians, new life in the Spirit has already begun. This does not mean that each new movement and renewal of the Spirit takes a wholly predictable course. Like the wind, the Spirit cannot be controlled or readily predicted (John 3.8). Nevertheless, as we have already noted in connection with the Spirit's revelation of truth, the Spirit's work remains coherent and self-consistent, and does not undermine or contradict what the Spirit has already achieved. While the future disclosed by the Spirit therefore outstrips all present conceiving or imagining, this future will not be at variance with those 'first instalments' of the Spirit which in Christ we have already received. ' "What no eye has seen, nor ear heard, nor the heart of man conceived, what God has prepared for those who love him" ', God has revealed to us through the Spirit. For the Spirit searches everything, even the depths of God' (1 Cor.2.9f.).

The image of the first fruits of the Spirit (Rom.8.23) conveys the truth that the present experience of the Holy Spirit is only the beginning, but nevertheless a real beginning, of the harvest proper which will come to ripened fruition in the future age. Until the harvest comes, the whole creation 'groans in travail' as it waits for this with eager longing. Paul feels the need to re-affirm his point that much of the centre of gravity still lies in the future: 'Now hope that is seen is not hope. For who hopes for what he sees?... We wait for it with

patience' (Rom.8. 24f.). But he also underlines the aspect of
continuity and promise. The first fruits of the Spirit come as a
partial bestowal in the present which guarantees a complete
bestowal in the future. This notion of guarantee is even more
explicit where Paul speaks of the Spirit as the assured pledge
that what God has destined will be fulfilled: 'He who has
prepared for us this very thing is God, who has given us the
Spirit as a guarantee' (2 Cor. 5.5). In a later epistle the idea of
guarantee is combined with that of a protective seal of authen-
ticity and safety: 'You ... were sealed with the promised Holy
Spirit, which is the guarantee of our inheritance until we
acquire possession of it' (Eph. 1.13f.). The same two ideas are
combined by Paul with reference to God's faithfulness to his
promise and commission to service. The Spirit here is given as
down-payment on what God has promised (2 Cor. 1.22). The
metaphor is that of a financial deposit which guarantees the
completion of the larger transaction. As God's own seal, the
Spirit marks out and protects a reality and identity which
would otherwise be only hidden or subject to ambiguity. The
Spirit pledges the completion of a process which the Spirit has
decisively set in motion.

Earlier in this chapter we concentrated on our future hope,
of which our present experience of the Spirit is both foretaste
and guarantee. Here we are seeking to explore more fully this
present experience. There is indeed both continuity and contrast between the present and the future, as can be seen in
other respects with regard to the Holy Spirit's work. The
Spirit prompts within us Jesus' own cry of trust and intimacy:
'Abba, Father' (Rom. 8.15; Gal. 4.6). Nevertheless sonship
reaches fullness in the future, for it carries with it, as we have
noted, a right to 'inheritance'. In Paul's language, 'It is the
Spirit himself bearing witness with our spirit that we are
children of God, and if children, then heirs, heirs of God and
fellow heirs with Christ' (Rom. 8.16f.). Because even heirs
wait for that which they inherit, the sufferings of Christ have
still to be shared, equally as a mark of the Spirit, and we 'who
have the first fruits of the Spirit groan inwardly as we wait for

adoption as sons' (Rom. 8.23). The emphasis here lies equally on the reality of the present and on the greater fullness of the future: 'He who sows to the Spirit will from the Spirit reap eternal life' (Gal. 6.8). Pentecost has already come, because God's love has already been 'poured into our hearts through the Holy Spirit' (Rom. 5.5). But 'we rejoice in our hope of sharing the glory of God', and even 'rejoice in our sufferings' (Rom. 5. 2f.), which now fall short of this future glory. With the whole of creation, we eagerly await our fuller freedom from bondage to decay, and fuller freedom of the children of God (Rom. 8.21). This yearning and longing is articulated within us by the Spirit 'with sighs too deep for words' (Rom. 8.26).

Can more be said, even indirectly through the use of symbols and imagery, about this future for which creation sighs? In the New Testament the 'last things' comprise the Parousia (or appearance of Christ in glory), the final judgement, and the general resurrection of the dead. These are cosmic or public events, rather than those which primarily concern the perceptions or hopes of the individual as such. In his book *In the End God* ... John Robinson rightly draws a contrast between the western individualism which focuses hope on the hour of death and the expectation of immortality, and the wider cosmic perspective of the New Testament which focuses hope on the day of the Parousia, the reality of the last judgement, and the event of the general resurrection. Creation longs for the coming of Christ in public vindication and glory. It longs for the dead to be raised, transformed and incorruptible, and yearns for the hidden ways of the Judge of all the earth to be made public and to be seen to set all wrongs to right. Judgement means the end of illusion and ambiguity; resurrection means the end of weakness and decay.

The New Testament attributes the resurrection of the dead directly to the agency of the Holy Spirit. Paul writes: 'If the Spirit of him who raised Jesus from the dead dwells in you, he who raised Christ Jesus from the dead will give life to your mortal bodies also through his Spirit which dwells in you'

(Rom. 8.11). If Christ himself is called the first fruits or firstborn of the resurrection order, the agency of the Spirit which raised Christ will raise those in Christ to share his resurrection mode of existence. The resurrection life of Christ and the future resurrection of Christians belong to a single process, initiated and sustained by the Holy Spirit. That the Spirit of God sustains the resurrection life was already anticipated figuratively in the Old Testament (Ezek.37). In Paul's great chapter on the resurrection (1 Cor. 15) the mode of existence demanded by the resurrection is itself 'spiritual' (1 Cor. 15.44), which is best interpreted to mean 'of the Holy Spirit'.

The immediate context of this verse confirms that 'spiritual' refers to that which is of the Holy Spirit. When he tells his readers that 'flesh and blood cannot inherit the kingdom of God' (1 Cor. 15.50), Paul is not addressing the Greek or western problem whether a physical entity can achieve a non-material, non-spatial, mode of existence. He is addressing the Hebrew-Christian problem whether an untransformed humanity, characterized by failure and sinfulness, can enter the immediate presence of God who is holy. Transformation through sharing in the resurrection of Christ is the key to hope. The Spirit has begun this process already, but the process culminates in a final decisive event. The whole person is raised imperishable. 'It is sown in dishonour, it is raised in glory. It is sown in weakness, it is raised in power' (1 Cor. 15.43). The *Revised Standard Version,* which we have followed elsewhere, misses the point of the contrast by translating the next verse 'It is sown a physical (Greek *psychikon*) body, it is raised a spiritual (Greek *pneumatikon*) body' (v.44). Paul uses the Greek word *psychikos* elsewhere in this epistle to denote the 'ordinary' or 'unspiritual' person in contrast to the person who is controlled or led by the Holy Spirit (1 Cor. 2.14). Hence it is more accurate to translate the word to mean 'ordinary'. The *New English Bible* translates this as 'animal' body. But our fully functional and fully operational mode of existence (equivalent for the biblical writers to 'body') will be characterized by the sustaining power of the Holy Spirit. Paul is not arguing here about the composition of the 'body', as if it were composed of (human) spirit; he is spelling out how the Holy Spirit transforms the Christian's mode of existence.

We should expect that a mode of existence animated and sustained by the Spirit of the living God would be conceived of in dynamic rather than in static terms. This is also implied by these verses. The process of decay or 'corruption' is reversed. Fine questions are raised about semantic contrasts here. It is likely that the opposite of decay is not simply lack of decay, but the very reversal of decay which we associate with rejuvenation, for the Spirit throughout the biblical writings is associated with strength and vitality. Paul consciously connects this with the completion of the process whereby the Christian is freed from the weakening and debilitating effects of sin, guilt and 'dishonour'. Behind the Greek word for decay stand the Hebrew words for what is marred and spoiled, and what is vain or fruitless. The spiritual mode of existence will not be like this: it will be fruitful, glorious and go on from strength to strength. The notion of a 'glorious body' is thus that of a fully operational and effective mode of existence, freed from weakening associations with sin, to enjoy an ongoing and progressive experience of life in the Spirit according to God's glory.

Nevertheless, neither resurrection nor judgement should be conceived of in over-individualistic terms. To be sure, the resurrection of the body affirms the value of the individual, in that it implies a future continuity of personal identity rather than a mere absorption of individuality into some all-encompassing whole. Judgement likewise underlines individual accountability and therefore individual identity. The Creator Spirit is the God of variety in creation, not of dull uniformity. However, the resurrection constitutes a cosmic event of renewal, for which all creation waits in travail. Is it merely speculative to suggest that this might be conceived by analogy with the transformation by which the human body is transposed into some transfigured mode of being? At very least, elsewhere in the New Testament the Seer beholds 'a new heaven and a new earth; for the first heaven and the first earth had passed away' (Rev. 21.1). He conveys a vision that when history as we know it has reached its end, a new arena or context of existence will be revealed. Into this new arena of existence are absorbed qualities of the present creation, albeit in transformed or transfigured modes. The new Jerusalem is prepared as a bride beautifully dressed for her wedding. A great voice said that God would dwell with his people; it went on, ' "He will wipe away every tear from their eyes, and death shall be no more, neither shall there be mourning nor crying nor pain any more, for the former things have passed away." And he who sat upon the throne said, "Behold, I make all things new" ' (Rev. 21. 4f.). This is the cosmic, public, and climactic fulfilment of the process already begun by the Spirit: 'We all, with unveiled face, beholding the glory of the Lord, are being changed into his likeness from one degree of glory to another; for this comes from the Lord who is the Spirit' (2 Cor. 3.18). This is the glory which even now fills 'the whole earth' (Is. 6.3).

The event of the resurrection, then, is a corporate event as well as one which involves us as individuals. The metaphor of the last trumpet conveys the idea of a sleeping army jumping to its feet when the signal is given. Judgement, equally, is both individual and cosmic. Creation yearns for that moment when the ways of God will receive visible and unequivocal vindication. Judgement means the end of ambiguity and illusion. God will be seen to be all in all.

The Holy Spirit begins this process of removing illusion now in the present. We have seen already that part of the Spirit's work as Paraclete is to convict us of sin and to expose those things which need forgiveness, transformation and healing (John 16. 8ff.). The Spirit brings the whole Church to judgement in advance by bringing home where we need the Spirit's defending and supporting help, and where there are failures that need to be corrected. The Spirit achieves this work in a variety of ways, including prayer, preaching, prophecy, theology and the witness of particular groups and persons. All this in principle brings forward aspects of divine judgement which will be revealed without ambiguity only at the last day. Meanwhile, it is because of this work of the Spirit at the individual level that we say to our Saviour Christ in a hymn, 'They who fain would serve thee best are conscious most of wrong within'.

We cannot yet conceive of the more detailed nature of this last judgement. We know that evil will be destroyed, but will human persons be caught up in destructive aspects of this decree? That evil attitudes on the part of persons will be destroyed is clear. The biblical and liturgical images of the Holy Spirit's activity as wind, as fire, and as water help us to see the two-sided nature of this work. Wind cools and refreshes, but it also blasts and destroys. Fire illuminates and warms, but it also burns. Water cleanses and purifies, but it may also submerge and drown. The new order will be a pure, untarnished realm. By definition, because it is pure and holy 'nothing unclean shall enter it' (Rev. 21.27). Those spiritual writers who, like Thomas à Kempis, Julian of Norwich, or Richard Baxter, speak most warmly of God's love also speak of the need to fear God's judgement. When this judgement is pronounced, all stand exposed in their final awareness of what they truly have been and are. Yet by the same token the plea for acceptance lies in nothing else than the grace and generosity of God's mercy as it is given and received through Christ. In Baxter's words, 'O terrible, O joyful, day!'

It is a different question whether God allows any human being or other creature finally to say 'no' to this generosity. Different traditions of Christian thought have answered this question in different ways. Some see the irresistible nature of grace in Pauline language about the reconciliation of all things: 'through him (Christ) to reconcile to himself all things, whether on earth or in heaven, making peace by the blood of his cross' (Col. 1.20). Others view this as expressing, rather, universal acceptance of the divine decree, whether of judgement or of mercy. Some see a reference to universal salvation in New Testament language about uniting 'all things in him (Christ), things in heaven and things on earth' (Eph.1.10). Others underline the wide range of possible meanings covered by the Greek word translated 'to unite' in the RSV *(anakephalaiō)*. At least one writer interprets this verse to mean that all things achieve a focus of meaning in Christ. Perhaps the biblical writers refrain from offering a neatly-packaged map of these last events because they function more strictly as an assurance of mercy to the humble and the seeking, and as a warning to the presumptuous, than as a piece of general information derived from some practical context.

In this sense, language about the last judgement is like the notoriously difficult verse about blasphemy against the Holy Spirit. Mark recounts the charge of some of the teachers of the law that Jesus was driving out demons by the prince of demons. Jesus replies that by its very nature and definition his work stands in conflict with that of Satan, and Mark attributes to him the saying: 'All sins will be forgiven the sons of men, and whatever blasphemies they utter; but whoever blasphemes against the Holy Spirit never has forgiveness, but is guilty of eternal sin' (Mk. 3.28f.). The saying stands as a warning against a wilful and deliberate manipulation of good and evil, by which evil is called 'good' and good is called 'evil' (cf. Is. 5.20). If a person were to manipulate all moral value and truth with such wilful cynicism, there is no way out of the vicious circle which has been erected. But Jesus does not mean a serious but hypothetical warning to be understood primarily as a general statement which is divorced from all context or questions of subjective concern. In everyday life, where people are concerned or deeply anxious about the possible applicability of this passage to their own lives, this very anxiety is itself full evidence that they do not share the callous cynicism and indifference to truth which this particular text addresses.

The same distinction between practical concern and general statement applies to language about the last judgement. Writers as strikingly different as Karl Barth and Julian of Norwich see the day of judgement as characterized equally by certainty and by hiddenness. Barth reminds us that God's grace and generosity is not limited by justice. Nevertheless, the person who persistently tries to change the truth into untruth 'cannot count on' God's eternal patience (K. Barth, *Church Dogmatics,* IV.3:1, p.477). In the late fourteenth and early fifteenth century Julian of Norwich wrote in a parallel way of the hiddenness and certainty of that day, and of how its nature and form would be determined by the goodness and love of God. She writes: 'What the deed will be and how it will be performed is unknown to every creature who is inferior to Christ, and it will be until the deed is done. The goodness and love of our Lord God want us to know that this will be, and his power and his wisdom, through the same love, want to conceal it and hide it from us, what it will be, and how it will be done ... through which deed he will make all things well' (Julian of Norwich, *Showings, Longer Text* ch. 32).

If we turn from the spiritual writings to philosophies of history, we may note that it is often said that the final significance of the events of our individual lives can be measured only in the hour of death. We must extend this principle corporately and trans-historically: only at the end of history will the full significance of historical moments be seen. The Holy Spirit, within the framework of faith, brings anticipation of this trans-historical perspective forwards to us in provisional forms (which are admittedly open to further elucidation and expansion). The Spirit does this for example in witnessing to our freedom from condemnation through Christ. The Holy Spirit also provides a witness that the individual is not alone in God's world, but is loved and valued along with all God's creation in heaven and on earth. This is a very different perspective from that of the secular futurologist who speculates about the future on the basis of extrapolations from the present. This more secular perspective fails to take account of the discontinuities and potential reversals which are implied by the notion of a last judgement. It represents a fragmented viewpoint which is caught up in a process of relativization, seeking to assess the future in the light of the present, rather than the present in the light of the future. The Holy Spirit has already revealed to faith enough of the 'last things' and of the Spirit's own part in them, to give us grounds for confident hope.

This hope for the future which is inspired by the Spirit moves beyond narrow concerns of self-interest and hopes of self-centred vindication. Creation yearns for an end to the power of all that is destructive. Love is the one quality which always abides and can never be left behind. In the present this is anticipated by a desire for change now, which begins with the transformation of the self in holiness and love, and shows itself in wider concerns for the world and society. Here the Spirit makes use of natural and scientific processes, but cannot be reduced to them exhaustively. For example, biology and medicine have increased life expectancy, but have thereby produced fresh problems of world population and scarcity of resources. Struggles to increase food supplies by chemical processes raise further difficulties about the control of bacteria and of related by-products. Yet amidst pain and suffering, the yearning of the Holy Spirit, as a divine discontent within, expresses itself in deeds of love, and longs for the future which God alone can bring. The final verse of Charles Wesley's hymn 'Love divine' sums up this longing:

> Finish then thy new creation, pure and spotless let us be;
> Let us see thy great salvation perfectly restored in thee.
> Changed from glory into glory, till in heaven we take our place,
> Till we cast our crowns before thee, lost in wonder, love, and praise.

Index of Biblical References

Old Testament

Index of Biblical References

Index of Biblical References

General Index

General Index